the Dark Voyage and the Golden Mean

A PHILOSOPHY OF COMEDY

ALBERT COOK

The Norton Library

W · W · NORTON & COMPANY · INC ·

NEW YORK

To   Dr. George Lee Phelps and Professor John H. Finley, Jr.,
*two teachers of scholarship, wisdom, and humanity
to whom I shall always owe what I understand of
Greek culture, and much else besides*

Published simultaneously in Canada by
George J. McLeod Limited, Toronto

Printed in the United States of America
1 2 3 4 5 6 7 8 9 0

Foreword

This book explores the philosophical meaning of art from the vantage point of comedy, the most complex and elusive, though not the most profound, aesthetic attitude. It proceeds by elucidating a group of technical terms, each of which symbolically contains the others. Though my thought could not have developed without the long tradition of kindred problems, I mention other critics only cursorily because in creating my own system, refuting or corroborating their ideas is a side issue.

The first two chapters explain my theory. The third chapter on Aristophanes is illustrative; each of the chapters which succeed it explores a different aspect of my idea to extend its meaning. I found it necessary to omit studies of writers whom I have long admired, read, and thought about; with particular regret I refrained from discussing Chaucer and Petronius. I know too little about Restoration comedy or Elizabethan comedy exclusive of Shakespeare to hazard writing about them. Plautus and Terence I neglect because I consider them overrated. Only the accident that Western Europe had nothing in the genre for a long time could have imparted such an undeserved reputation to works so devoid of ideas. The brilliance of many modern critics has done ample justice to Chaplin's comedy.

My personal debts are great. John Finley at one time or another has touched on almost every point in this book; suffice it to say that I have borrowed from him such key ideas as the rationalism of allegory, the concept–symbol struggle in fifth-century Athens, and the comparison of the *Odyssey* to *The Tempest*. The theories of George Kingsley Zipf have united many diverse ideas for me. In addition to contributing many specific insights, Thomas McFarland has broadened my basic ideas by discussing them with me and has made numerous valuable suggestions about the manuscript. I owe thanks also to Professor Finley, John

Brown, Eugene Pantzer, Professor C. R. Post, Mrs. Cedric Whitman, and Mr. Thomas J. Wilson of the Harvard University Press for reading the manuscript, for suggestions and encouragement. My wife Carol has given me much aid in addition to preparing the index.

ALBERT COOK

Old Forge, New York
July, 1948.

> *If we desire to formulate an accurate theory of poetry, we find it necessary to examine the structure of reality, because reality is the central reference for poetry.*
>
> —WALLACE STEVENS

> *When, therefore, in the present work also, precedence is given to Time, Direction and Destiny over Space and Causality, this must not be supposed to be the result of reasoned proofs. It is the outcome, of (quite unconscious) tendencies of life-feeling—the only mode of origin of philosophic ideas.*
>
> —SPENGLER

> *Wer je die flamme umschritt*
> *Bleibe der flamme trabant!*
> *Wie er auch wandert und kreist*
> *Wo noch ihr schein ihn erreicht*
> *Irrt er zu weit nie vom ziel.*
> *Nur wenn sein blick sie verlor*
> *Eigener schimmer ihm truegt:*
> *Fehlt ihm der mitte gesetz,*
> *Treibt er zerstiebend ins all.*
>
> —STEFAN GEORGE

Contents

Other Books by Albert Cook

The Meaning of Fiction
Oedipus Rex: A Mirror for Greek Drama (Editor and Translator)
Progressions (Poems)
The Classic Line: A Study of Epic Poetry
The Odyssey (Translation)
Prisms: Studies in Modern Literature

THE PROBABLE AND THE WONDERFUL

*The great problem of literature is to invent a
probability and make it wonderful.*

—DRYDEN

*Denn das Schöne ist nichts
als des Schrecklichen Anfang.*

—RILKE

However man may will or desire otherwise, his life falls into patterns of probability; and even the turning of the sun in night and day, the cycle of the seasons, the biological course of human life are only the scene of his probable actions. The very economy of material existence ordains that most of us will occupy similar houses in a similar horizon, tread similar paths to and from our daily work, eat similar dishes and beget similar children. This is true for social groups; the American bourgeois (or Turkish rich man, or Arab camel driver, or Greek philosopher) sufficiently resembles other members of his class in appearance, thought, and action, to be considered a type. And it is true for the individual, whose daily acts repeat themselves to become his probable habits, so that he arises about the same time from about the same bed, performs about the same acts during the day, thinks, feels, dreams, reads things similar to those of yesterday. These acts are never the same. That would be closed certainty, the fixed act in the fixed cosmos. And nature abhors stasis. You are not the same man that fell asleep a while ago, and it is not the same bed. But you and the bed are very like the ones that last night, as the moon rose, were borne in the flow of experiential time. Your friends still recognize you, and you still recognize the bed. From the norms of the probable there is no escape. There are voyagers, but do they not all go in like vessels, travel like courses, stay in like inns? And is not the stranger a social type?

So our physical scene, governed without by the sun and within by the growth and decay of our bodies.

So the objects in that scene—houses, trees, tables, chairs, men, cats. These are types; otherwise how would I know that Socrates is a man, that 15 Main Street is a house?

So the motions—walking, hammering, eating.

So the acts—birth, marriage, murder, pleading, creation.

So the mind of the agent—the optimist, the schizoid, the visionary, the kind father. This is in the realm of *pure action,* without reference to the philosophic system in which the type we recognize is classified. The

3

choleric man is as valid a type in our experience as the Electra woman, whatever the superiority of Freud's psychology to Aristotle's.

So the effect on the mind of the agent—fear, anxiety, delight, conviction.

In reality as we live it, in the pure unconscious action of existence, in our profoundest experiences, our deepest traumas, our most towering intellectual systems, the order of the norm can be traced no less than in our trade routes, our customs, our languages.

As the norm lies in one lifetime, so can it be traced in the economic course of a community or the political course of a nation (in Pareto's income curves, for example, or in statistics on social mobility). Hegel and Spengler have found the norm in the spiritual course of a culture, Jung in the inner life of the human race, Heraclitus and Blake in the fire of the universe which is in perpetual flower. All is probable. There is nothing new under the sun.

RATIONALES OF THE PROBABLE · INDUCTIVE REASONING

Whether or not man is self-conscious, the norm exists for him in the pure action of his experience. When he turns in contemplation to the multitude of *facts* about him (scenes, objects, agents, actions, states of mind) he finds ordered groups in them, which he classifies as types. There is a type "plant," beneath that a type "tree," beneath that again a type "elm," and finally an object that grows in his own backyard, unique, though it possesses most of its characteristics in common with other trees.

The method of numerically arranging these groups of facts, especially social facts, has developed in recent history as the science of statistics. It diagrams the probable on the bell curve, where most of the individuals in the group are clustered around the mean, and their frequency decreases as the curve (hence the group) nears either extreme.

To proceed from these ordered groups of facts to a general idea, one uses the technique of *inductive* reasoning. The body of laws governing this technique constitute *logic,* which, like statistics, has advanced much in the past century by the use of mathematics.

Combining one general *induced* idea with another is dialectic. It is important not to confuse this process with deduction. As will be shown, the probable is social, wherefore it is peculiarly apt that dialectic has most often been employed in connection with the history and management of society.

RATIONALES OF THE PROBABLE · DEDUCTIVE REASONING

Reasoning by logic from premises instead of from facts is deduction. The sole difference between induction and deduction is the starting point—fact or premise. But in deduction the premise is assumed to be a fact. Therefore all logical reasoning is the arrangement of facts, as defined above, either experienced (as in induction) or assumed (as in deduction). The probable, which exists in the ordered groups of facts in human experience, can be examined and meaningful conclusions drawn from it. Reason, deductive or inductive, is the sole technique for drawing these conclusions. *All thought on the probable is rationalistic.* This explains why the development of logic and the development of the philosophy of probability have always gone hand in hand. Aristotle, the great philosopher of the probable, developed logic; our own epoch, which revolutionized logic, has also greatly concerned itself with the philosophy of probability. Statistics is only one manifestation of this; others will be discussed later.

THE DESIRE FOR THE NONPROBABLE

Man desires change because it is pleasurable. As he makes his way through a probable world anything he meets which is nonprobable—change of place, diet, sexual partner, ideas, reading matter, job—stimulates him in direct proportion to its nonprobability. Novelty is always surprising, therefore unpredictable, therefore nonprobable. But probability is the lot of man, however he strives to avoid it. With what expectation do we wait for the daily mail, hoping that the official communications from our cosmos will thrust through in the form of a letter with the essence of wonder! Always, no matter what the letter may contain, there is a vague disappointment, a metaphysical ennui. It is the intuitive perception of the probable as the channel of all limited human experience, and

5

therein the desire to be a god, the yearning for the infinite, is thwarted.

The ways to seek novelty are legion, and they always end in disappointment. The searcher at the end of his road finds himself staring the probable in the face. The boy who runs away from dull school to the sea which he imagines is ever-changing soon discovers that he has arranged for himself a stale probability of endless water, filth of foreign harbors, prostitutes, and violent escape through drink. His counterpart on land, the tramp, seeks to break up the normal pattern of a laboring day. But where is freedom, where is change, in the endless shift across the "empire wilderness of freight and rails"? Begging bread, brewing mulligan stews, policing hobo jungles, dodging police—these are probabilities even more wearing than working eight hours a day on a machine.

Most men make voyages on occasion; only the seeker is always on the move. So, while many men indulge in sex with new partners on occasion, only the seeker continually strives for new conquests. His motives may vary. Casanova's avowed purpose was to "tromper les sots." The main aim of his conquests was revenge on society (*les sots*) for some imagined wrong, not the search for the nonprobable. Don Juan, on the other hand, was the aesthete of experience, the searcher for the wonderful, the voyager into the country which was perpetually new. This, not his mere physical prowess or social adroitness, explains the fascination he has held for first-rate artists, among them Molière, Mozart, and Kierkegaard. But Bernard Shaw, in trying to make him a great thinker, commits the error of imagining him a success. He who seeks novelty in seducing a thousand women finds himself seducing the same woman a thousand times. Women, like men, are largely alike. They are predictable, therefore probable, in sex. The Don Juan who starts out to be titillated ends by being jaded. There emerges finally what he sought to avoid, the probable, staler than even he would have found it in normal life. Casanova in his *Memoirs* ceaselessly advises against this course, and his advice was not the result of senility. As with change of sexual partner, so with change of mode of sexual experience. One gets off easiest with a dull bestiality; usually there results the ennui of intolerable detachment.

Death, though probable for man, is nonprobable for the individual.

Only once can it occur, and with it the destruction of the earthly self, the great change from material life to either annihilation or eternity. Cheap literature, which always contains the nonprobable in childish forms (like a love affair, wonderfully new yet morally sound), often represents death as occurring twice, as in the childbirth experience of the girl in *Our Town*. There have been those who have sought sure death directly as a complete change of state. It is said that the suicide seeks not so much self-annihilation, since he is usually egotistical, as an entirely new experience. He wishes to redefine his cosmos completely. This explains the love of Tristan and Isolde, which de Rougemont in *Love in the Western World* has associated with supreme love of ego and death-wish. It is no accident that the dramatist of this love was the dramatist of the great heroic voyagers, Siegfried and Parsifal.

Since death is usually nonprobable, when it becomes probable, as in battle, fear is aroused. Fear, like pleasure, results from the presence of the unpredictable, of sudden change. Because of this it is not altogether unpleasurable. Hence there are cultists who seek fear as a means of achieving the unpredictable nonprobable. By placing the self in danger, in the realm where death is likely to occur at any moment, one calls to life the masculine self. The presence of death acts as catalyst between the ego and the core of life; one becomes a hero and achieves the continual thrill of the wonderful. Bullfighting or big-game hunting can serve this purpose, but its best instrument is battle. Here Ernest Hemingway is a mewling babe in a company which includes Storm Trooper aesthetes and General Patton, who wrote verse to the "God of Battles" and was so single-minded that he saw no difference between Nazism and American political parties. It is consistent that such men are often Don Juans to boot. But when death is always imminent, it becomes probable. The *pleasure* of fear arises only from its infrequency. When it becomes normal it gets dull. At best, the effect is brutality; at worst, tics, stomach ulcers, loss of limbs, or early death.

THE SEARCH FOR THE WONDERFUL

There are tramps and sailors, Don Juans and professional soldiers, who do not seek the nonprobable. Yet those who do seek, even the most childish escapists, are more sensitive than those who do not—and more intelligent. Terman, in *Genetic Studies of Genius,* cites the case of a boy whose I.Q. was among the highest he studied, who burned himself out in a few years on the seas. In a sociological study of tramps, the University of Chicago found that I.Q.'s of 130 and above in their group are more than twice as frequent as in the general population. This is not usually true of prostitutes, a superficially analogous pariah group. There is deep significance in Hart Crane's fascination with sailors and with tramps, whom he considered the last pioneers; in Picasso's *Les Saltimbanques;* in the life of Rimbaud; in Sinbad the Sailor and Ulysses in both folk motif and Joyce.

Granted that the bullfighters, the tramps, the Don Juans fail; what can be said of deeper searchers for the wonderful, the artist and the saint? Only ego-identification, seeing the tramp's inner similarity to himself, can explain the artist's fascination with these ill-starred pariahs and his sympathy for them. He does not have to take dope like Francis Thompson and DeQuincey to sympathize with and befriend a sensitive prostitute; nor roam like Rimbaud to contemplate the sailor; nor be a profligate to understand the temptation and fall of Don Juan, as Molière and Mozart testify.

Much has been said of the artist (or saint) and his madness, the wound that makes him prize the bow of his art. The artist's life follows the neurotic pattern of abnormal need for affection, an instability caused by psychic starvation or abnormal suffering. From the probable, social, psychological point of view, it is this anxiety that drives him out of the normal path into the search for the wonderful. So they are, artist and saint, both deranged, both inward, both heedlessly on the same lonely road of search for the wonderful where the childish tramp has foundered. Whether they seek *le dérèglement de tous les sens* like Rimbaud, or are moral but poor like Joyce, socially they must be pariahs. Almost always they are failures in the eyes of the world. At best they are thought odd ducks. Nothing is more incongruous in any society than the artist who is its pillar. Either he is misunderstood, or he is considered a priest, as in

8

Greece. (The priest, of course, is an officially nonprobable outsider.)

To deny that Rimbaud's early family life or Dostoievsky's father problem and tribulations brought about the existence and tone of their work is to deny both their essential humanity and art's roots in life. On the other hand, to think that this efficient cause, neurosis, completely explains the art, is to turn all art into clinical data. This is a materialistic fallacy. Freud steered between both errors, saying in *Totem and Taboo:*

> In one way the neuroses show a striking and far-reaching correspondence with the great social productions of art, religion and philosophy, while again they seem like distortions of them. We may say that hysteria is a caricature of an artistic creation; a compulsion neurosis, a caricature of a religion; and a paranoiac delusion, a caricature of a philosophic system.

Othello is abnormally susceptible to jealousy, and an adventurer, because he is an outsider (the black Moor), and vice versa. Oedipus both solved the riddle of the Sphinx and married his mother.

This is why Mary Magdalene, though a prostitute, could be converted so easily. Of those to whom much is given, much will be required. The act of becoming a pariah and falling into the most grievous sins of the flesh was more likely for her because she was born sensitive. But the sensitive person, though more susceptible to sin, is also more capable of divine understanding, of repenting and taking the religious way. He is not hampered by the bourgeois habits that stifle change to the good; neither is he helped, till he wills them, by the habits of a religious life. The scales are still justly balanced between inclination for good and inclination for evil. For the searcher, it takes a more delicate weight to make them incline.

The searcher deliberately drives himself away from the normal experience of humankind to the probability of abnormality. But he also proceeds toward a more satisfying mode of life, one with more love; even, in a sense, with more stability. He desires distinction in the double sense of separateness from the crowd and love by the crowd. The ambiguity of the single word is the ambiguity of his unified act and the ambiguity of his sickness/abnormal health. The word "dangerous" in Middle English meant "standoffish because of high social class." The shift of meaning becomes clear when the concepts of probability and its converse nonprobability are introduced.

The sepulchre must ope its ponderous and marble jaws, the probable be turned topsy-turvy, and great psychic wounds be incurred for Hamlet to waken from the active dream of a courtier's life to his profound search for the meaning of existence. Yet the probable in the form of outraged brother (Laertes) and unscrupulous rival (Claudius) killed him while he was still committing unnecessary errors—for example, venting on the innocent Ophelia his stored-up hatred for his betrayal (in the sexual, Oedipus sense) by his mother. When the action of this nonprobable family had played itself out in exploring the human psyche, the probable in the form of rationally organized power (Fortinbras) took over. Norway is equal in macrocosm (national power) to the microcosmic group of Gertrude, Claudius, Polonius, Laertes, and Ophelia (family social pressure).

Lear is the tragedy of one who has lived so long in the probable mask of polite social life that he is unable to understand the terrible, nonprobable action that life can give. The gradual realization cracks him under its tremendous weight. In the course of the play he is transformed by outward adversity and inward breakdown from a king who confidently gives orders at the beginning to a poetic prophet in the last act:

> No, no, no, no! Come, let's away to prison;
> We two alone will sing like birds i' th' cage.
> When thou dost ask me blessing, I'll kneel down
> And ask of thee forgiveness. So we'll live,
> And pray, and sing, and tell old tales, and laugh
> At gilded butterflies, and hear poor rogues
> Talk of court news; and we'll talk with them too,
> Who loses and who wins; who's in, who's out;
> And take upon 's the mystery of things
> As if we were God's spies; and we'll wear out,
> In a wall'd prison, packs and sects of great ones
> That ebb and flow by th' moon.

10

Or he is a man cast in the wrong role; if—which would have been probable—Lear had been more suited to his job or his job to him, he would have died peacefully. The question of role recurs often, as in the Fool's statement to Lear, "I am a fool, thou art nothing," where Lear's loss of type and function equals social annihilation; or in Edgar's symbolic assumption of madness when he is changed from the role of young nobleman to that of outcast, "Edgar I nothing am."

Society always condemns, casts out, or castrates its artists and saints. The social, probable, conceptual thinker provides a system wherein the nonsocial searcher is transformed into the antisocial menace. Society, the crowd, crucified the Saviour of the World on two sound rationalist principles: that one man should die for the preservation of order (Caiaphas), and that all truth is relative to its postulates. What is truth? asked Pilate. Probable, quoth the rationalist. What could be more nonprobable than that one of the thousands who claim at one time or another to be divine should actually be so? What is less rationalistic than simple assertions, having no demonstrable foundation in fact, not even grounded on postulates? Yet the saint and the artist are guilty of illogic only from the point of view of rationalism. They work in the realm of revelation and symbol, not of premise and conclusion. Theirs the wonderful, not the probable. Rationally they are nonprobable; symbolically they are revealed as true.

It is only incidental that the wonderful can be stated in rationalist terms. Saint Thomas professed that his rationalistic edifice was only the superficial pattern of the *revelabile*. Its essence was suprarational religious truth. Wallace Stevens says that Thomism is a function of prodigious logic and prodigious love of God. But the love is beginning and end, the logic only an instrument. Plato's Idea is supralogical and wonderful. Of Kierkegaard's three levels—aesthetic, ethical, and religious—only the first two are perceptible in rationalistic terms; faith alone can understand the last. *Credo ut intelligam* means not just the intellectual acceptance of logical postulates, but the imaginative faith of the soul which imbues a rationalist train of argument with its ideal meaning.

It is the artist, thinking through symbol, not concept, who has so

11

eagerly embraced these philosophers of the wonderful, Plato, Kierke-gaard. They are imaginative thinkers and to understand them only as builders of logical edifices is to miss their whole meaning.

THE PROBABLE AND THE WONDERFUL

We are dealing with two profoundly different techniques for attacking human experience: the probable and the wonderful. These terms them-selves, as suggested above, imply other, related antinomies: rationalism–idealism, society–artist, concept–symbol, society–individual. The prob-able–wonderful antinomy need not be taken as the focal point for this complex of dual oppositions. Any other of these would serve the same purpose. The one commonly used is the reason–imagination antinomy, or, in Bergson's terms, extensive and intensive manifolds. *We have shifted the base from the epistemological problem (reason–imagination) to the objects-as-perceived (probable–wonderful),* in order to bring out more clearly that the points of view are opposed and that, as each implies the other, they focus the ambiguity of all thought.

REASON VERSUS IMAGINATION

Reason, the logical faculty, attempting to synthesize a multitude of facts which are similar in some respects and dissimilar in others, will resolve upon the typical and probable as meaningful for life. But imagination enshrines the ideal, the wonderful, supralogical insight into the true nature of reality.

To reason (the probable) imagination seems merely the glitter on the intricate web woven by the retreating ego. To imagination (the wonder-ful) reason seems a superficial pattern of experience. Of Plato's three levels of perception—name (*onoma*), reason (*logos*), and form (*eidos*)—the last, which equals imagination, is the truth. Reason, the second, is only a step on the way to the grasp of form.

SOCIETY AND THE INDIVIDUAL

All social thought is probable. In the art of government as understood by

12

Machiavelli or Thucydides, the probable of pure action is the guiding principle. Experience presents individual cases (*facts*) that form themselves into a norm which is used as a guide in future dealings. Manners, like government, are simply norms of past experience, the probable as pure action. There is no philosophy involved in holding a fork, dressing for dinner, or piloting a woman comfortably through an evening at the theater. One knows what has been normal in the past in one's society. One does it, assuming that probably it is the course of least shock (intrusion of the nonprobable) to one's companions. As manners are social, so an ethical system is individual, a point which will be discussed later in connection with the philosophical basis of comedy and tragedy.

When the social thinker approaches the norms of pure action in social phenomena, he employs deduction and induction. Reason discovers the norms by which the government can best be managed, and rationalist analysis of pure-action norms is the basic technique of law. Economics uses induction and statistics (rationales of the probable); sociology and psychology add thereto the human case history, in which they try to delineate norms. The problems of these social sciences are meaningfully attacked by the accumulation of facts, the ordered arrangement of them, and inductions therefrom—in short, by cases, statistics, and reason. The probable is social, both in pure action (manners, statesmanship) and in rationale (economics, psychology, sociology).

Imagination is the technique of those who probe the soul of the individual man—the saint and the artist. Revealed religion and art make discoveries through the wonderful window of the soul. The rationalist statement of their meaning is only superficial description, even in ethics. For the greatest ethical philosophers—Plato, Augustine, Nietzsche, and Kierkegaard—have been imaginative, even when their discourse is rationalistic. Finally, the supreme ethical prophets are purely religious figures: Christ, Buddha, Isaiah, all mystics; and minor prophets have been artists, like Blake and Rousseau. Aristotle, who stresses pure action, pleasure as the highest good, and the philosophy of the mean, is social and probable. He discusses not ethics but manners. Even in the psychology of the individual, the great thinkers have been intuitive. Freud's ideas

13

are not inductive; case histories suggested them only in the same sense that life experience suggests to the artist.

Ego, id, superego, libido; totem and taboo; the discussions of wit; the Oedipus, Electra, and castration complexes—these are imaginative units, symbols arrived at by insight, not by deductive or inductive reason. The interpretation of dreams proceeds by analysis of symbols, as does the criticism of art. It treats of the symbols in the dream as an imaginative critic treats of the symbols in a poem. The idea of anxiety (*Angst*) borders on religious thought; and it has been discussed by Kierkegaard and Spengler in terms of imagination as a problem of the individual soul. Gestalt, which stresses the ideal whole that one makes of his experience, is closer to Platonic idealism than to Behaviorist rationalism. The same may be said of Jung's archetypes. These two psychologies have been consistently misunderstood by many rationalist thinkers, including some professional psychologists. Reason is probable and impersonal, therefore social; imagination is wonderful and personal, therefore individual.

EMPIRICISM · INDUCTION · DEDUCTION

The probable is empirical in the pure action of habit, diplomacy, manners, any predictable situation. It is inductive when reasoning from fact to idea, in dialectic, the social sciences, and so on. When premises are considered to be facts, it can be deductive.

These are logical categories, and therefore alien to the nature of the wonderful. But if the wonderful is seen from the rationalist (probable) point of view, they may be applied. Empirically, in pure action, the wonderful manifests itself as ideal symbol. A tree is a probable fact, but the Mystic Rose is a wonderful symbol; what is more, a tree—probable fact in the context of the botanist or rationalist philosopher—can act as wonderful symbol in a work of the imagination—a poem or a painting. Deductively, the wonderful is *a priori* thought. God is postulated, and His attributes are considered through the screen of rational dialectic.

But this is through the eyes of the probable. In the probable there is a clear distinction between action (the habit of selling) and thought (the rationale of economics). In the wonderful, no such distinction exists. *The wonderful is at once thought and action.* Faith in God and the *a priori* idea of God, having a mystic vision and symbolically understanding the mystic vision, are one and the same thing. It follows that only those who have *acted* the wonderful in their own imaginations will accept the foregoing *conceptual* account of it. Kenneth Burke sees literature as symbolic action. So it is, but it is symbolic thought also, and the two are identical. Of course I do not speak of the realm of physical action or moral action, where ethics should apply, but only of empirical pure action, which is different from both.

THE PROBABLE'S VIEW OF THE WONDERFUL

There are some men who have perceived that symbolic thinkers are great thinkers, yet commit the subtlest error of all in considering them as conceptual thinkers off on a tangent. When Shaw maintains that visions are a valid way of getting concepts, he thinks he is vindicating the saint, whereas actually he is destroying the real basis of the saint's thought. Mark Schorer's recent book on Blake falls into this same error. Schorer's line is that Blake was a great philosopher, but was deluded about his visions. His ego at that time in history had to veil the ideas in visionary form and his greatest error was attributing to God the peculiar mechanisms of his psychological needs. The classic case of this form of mistake is Aristotle's view of Plato. Werner Jaeger, in his introduction to *Aristotle,* calls those men pettifogging who say that Aristotle misunderstood Plato, for Aristotle studied under Plato for over twenty years, admired him greatly, and, though surpassing him conceptually, respected the doctrine of Ideas enough to give intuition (*epagogé*) a high place in his system. Precisely. Aristotle committed the error of Schorer and Shaw.

TRANSFORMATIONS · THE WONDERFUL AS PROBABLE

This tension between wonderful seeing itself as symbol and probable seeing it as *a priori* thought has borne much fruit in philosophy and art. To the religious man, the wonderful is the supreme probable; if all is seen *sub specie aeternitatis*. Blake, Heraclitus, and the Indian cosmic cycle are cases in point. And the rationalist account of revelation is material for philosophy, as in the works of the wonderful philosophers discussed above, Kierkegaard, Saint Thomas, and Plato. When a pure *a priori* pattern is superimposed on the symbol, art like the music of Bach or Byzantine mosaics can result. Such art is superbly unified because the *a priori* rational pattern and the symbol are the same thing seen from the different points of view of reason and imagination. To Plato *only* the wonderful was completely probable. The Idea was pure norm, and all else was seen through a jaundiced eye.

TRANSFORMATIONS · THE PROBABLE AS WONDERFUL

The *a priori* thought—symbol tension can be seen from the point of view of the wonderful, when a pure *a priori* system, like mathematics, is transformed into a symbol. There result such ideas as the "music of the spheres" or the "spirituality" of mathematics. Blake would write *"music* of the spheres," Gauss, "music of the *spheres,"* with a difference of focus.

PROBABLE TO NONPROBABLE · THE DEGREE OF PREDICTABILITY

How predictable a philosopher considers human existence to be is basic to his philosophy. Whether you assume that society can or cannot be rational, that life is or is not happy, that the soul is or is not addicted to evil, makes all the difference in the world, even in rationalist terms. The efficient cause of a philosopher's position here can be the disruption of his age, the sorrow of his life, or both. Plato saw the saintly Socrates go to death, the Athenian State defeated, ruthless opportunists progress in politics, his own Utopian trials in Sicily fail. Though he believed in the good life, he doubted man's capacity to govern himself sanely. Like Sophocles, he was a tragic optimist who believed in reconciliation with life after great suffering. The focus of Aristotle, essentially safe in his graduate school, was entirely different. Men are probable and predictable to Aristotle. Abuses in the slavery system, a natural order, are only occasional. Man has a capacity for intemperance, but it can be handled by the formation of a moral habit (*hexis*), by common sense.

Consider the difference between Kierkegaard and Mill. The great Christian lived in a universe of perpetually unforeseeable temptation, yawning abysses of sin, the tremendous calculus of guilt. The Utilitarian thought everything predictable, if men would only be reasonable. The basic difference is how predictable each thinks events are and how capable men are to govern themselves sanely. Kierkegaard's view is wonderful, individual, based on faith; Mill's is probable, social, based on reason.

It has often been remarked that the nonprobability of events in France during the last decade gave rise to the pessimistic Existentialism, which believes lonely man to be at large in an unpredictable universe. Contrast the Existentialist ontology, which denies classes, types, generalities (probabilities) of any kind, with the Thomistic, which is based on essence, substance, matter, form—and after the Realists and the Nominalists had been at it for three centuries. To Saint Thomas, death is a critical change of status for the soul, but its nature remains the same. To the Existentialists, as to the pessimistic Lucretius (whom they strongly resemble), the whole meaning of life is fundamentally bound to death-as-annihilation. One of their number, Camus, even ventured the statement that the problem of suicide is the basic problem of all philosophy. They admire Kierkegaard, not because he is a Christian, but because he is an individualist and because his focus is in nonpredictability.

Probability ranges from near certainty through likelihood to nonforeseeable possibility. This is a question of degree, and where a philosophy stands therein can determine its whole character. Individual philosophers may equate the nonprobable with the wonderful and transform it again to the wonderful-as-probable. When one makes this transformation and another does not, and both believe life to be unpredictable, strange bedfellows may result; for example, Kierkegaard and the Existentialists.

PHILOSOPHIES OF MEAN AND EXTREME

Some philosophies, grounded in the probable, call for the norm as the guide of life. Nothing to excess; don't play golf, be religious, read

17

philosophy, spend money, make friends, esteem yourself—too much or too little. Vice is either excess or deficiency of virtue, which itself is the middle road, the Aristotelian golden mean. Man should concern himself with spending wisely, avoiding unpleasantness, keeping up his station in peace and war, running his business well, caring for the family—in short, with all *social* (probable) activities. Ethos (ἦθος, τὰ ἠθικά, subject of the *Ethics*) in the Aristotelian sense is accumulating experience to form a group of habits (*habitus, hexis*) till one acquires a character type (ἦθος). The sphere of human activity is society and its form *pure action,* whereby all *thought* applies to it only roughly (παχυλῶς). Aristotle dismisses the nonprobable from his system; he refuses to consider it. In order to affirm the self-sufficiency of man, he denies an unpredictable range of possibility of events. To him, the tragic event—imprisonment, slavery, torture, murder, sin—is nonprobable and therefore not to be considered in "ethics."

How different from Christianity, the whole meaning of which revolves around our conduct in the face of extreme events! Indeed, in Christian ethics, all events are extreme moral crises, tinged with temptation. One ideal principle, love, guides the individual in his ego-involvements with other individuals. To the Christian it is not reprehensible to be laughed at or degraded in the eyes of society, whereas to the Aristotelian disgrace is synonymous with failure. What matters to the Christian is cleansing the soul, nearness to good and to God, the performance of ideally good acts. Though Christianity tries to harness the probable in the form of religious habits, it is the prototype of the philosophy of the extreme; Aristotelianism, of the philosophy of the mean.

Predictability, discussed above, is a question of degree. But the question of choice between mean and extreme is one of kind. Kierkegaard with his unpredictable universe could understand the predictable Saint Thomas. The Hindu (or Christian) extremist mystic appears as absurd to the sophisticated Molière or Aristophanes as the sophisticate appears damned to the mystic.

Machiavellians, gallants, followers of Confucius, are philosophers of the mean; drunkards, dandies, all searchers for the wonderful, are philosophers of the extreme. One misleading search for extreme in novelty is Pater's: "To burn always with this hard gemlike flame . . . is success in life." Yet how does the mind or body so burn, except by the constant reception of novel stimuli? Pater's ideal is perpetual anxiety, the search for the wonderful debased into aestheticism. On the other hand, there are some modern materialists who, equipped with a subtle technique for examining personality patterns, conceive all "cure" in terms of adjustment to as near the norm as possible. If you are abnormal, you are diseased; if normal, cured. The ideological connections between mean–extreme philosophies and comedy–tragedy will be treated later.

CLASSICISM AND ROMANTICISM

The terms classicism and romanticism do not have any ultimate rationalist meaning expressible in other, conceptual terms. Like the signs "probable" and "wonderful" as used in this essay, they are symbols for two different ways of regarding art. They can only be explored, never explained.

Norm and "nature" (in the sense of the predictable probable, the "natural") are always stressed in the critical discussions of classicists. Classic, by derivation, means exemplar or norm. Aristotle preferred a "probable impossible" (a technically impossible fact or act which represents the norm) to an "improbable possible" (a nonrepresentative *fait accompli*). On the probable are based Boileau's cult of *vraisemblance* and English classical criticism in the eighteenth century. As Pope said, "Those rules of old, discovered, not devised, were nature still, but nature methodized," (where "methodized" equals "rationalized into types or norms"). *Decorum* is a key word in Latin rationalist criticism. It means the avoidance of coupling two objects or events not habitually (probably) associated with each other, a use fully consistent with its later use in manners, the probable empiricism of social action.

Because the wonderful is seen rationally as nonprobable, critical theory reacting against classicism may react against the probable. Men who seek novel experience and stress individual rights in ethics substitute the exploring of personal life for classical patterns of human experience. Art becomes subjective or "romantic" instead of objective or "classic." Yet

19

the romanticist of the nonprobable may remain a rationalist. Shelley, a dabbler in science, espoused the rationalistic Godwinism. Like Wordsworth, he saw in nature an implicit order which relieved man of the necessity of creating order for himself. (Thomas McFarland points this out in "Proust: The Philosophic Implications of Classicism," *Halcyon*, Winter, 1948).

Different from the rationalist, nonprobable romantics are the wonderful romantics, who stress the imagination, the symbol, the eternal present. This difference is clearly explained in Kenneth Burke's brilliant analysis of the "Ode on a Grecian Urn" (*Grammar of Motives,* p. 449):

> *Heard melodies are sweet, but those unheard*
> *Are sweeter; therefore, ye soft pipes, play on;*
> *Not to the sensual ear, but, more endear'd*
> *Pipe to the spirit ditties of no tone:*
> *Fair youth, beneath the trees, thou canst not leave*
> *Thy song, nor ever can those trees be bare;*
> *Bold Lover, never, never canst thou kiss,*
> *Though winning near the goal—yet, do not grieve;*
> *She cannot fade, though thou hast not thy bliss,*
> *Forever wilt thou love, and she be fair.*

Contrast Keats' unheard melodies with those of Shelley:—

Music, when soft voices die,
Vibrates in the memory—
Odours, when sweet violets sicken,
Live within the sense they quicken.

Rose leaves, when the rose is dead,
Are heaped for the beloved's bed;
And so thy thoughts, when thou art gone,
Love itself shall slumber on.

Here the futuristic Shelley is anticipating retrospection; he is looking forward to looking back. The form of thought is naturalistic and temporalistic in terms of *past* and *future*. But the form of thought in Keats is mystical, in terms of an *eternal present*. The Ode is striving

to move beyond the region of becoming into the realm of *being.*
(Italics Burke's.)

Blake and Coleridge share with Keats this belief in imagination, the symbol, the wonderful. Consistent with this is the deep religiosity of Blake and the concern of Coleridge with guilt as a theological problem (recently traced by Robert Penn Warren). These poets are at least as different from the other romantics as they are from the classicists, and this difference has played hob with critics who try to define romanticism to include both. This was observed by Hegel, who traces a development similar to the above—*thesis:* classicism (the probable); *antithesis:* romanticism (nonprobable rationalism, Shelley); *synthesis:* symbolism (the wonderful, imagination). Symbolism as a synthesis includes both imagination and reason, with the former as the higher function. Therefore symbolism in this sense does not exclude but transcends classicism.

NATURALISM AND SYMBOLISM

These two great aesthetic movements of our time do not differ in rational basis from the classic–romantic antinomy. Naturalism, as selection of typical social events, equals classicism. Symbolism, like romanticism, can be either fanciful, as with the Surrealists, or imaginative, as with Mann, Kafka, Eliot. The difference is great, however, between the twentieth century and its predecessors. Ours is more willing to face the existence of evil, and is more pessimistic because the dichotomy between artist and society has become explicit, both financially and ideologically. How profoundly lonely and sour are these lines in *Bateau Ivre:*

> *Toute lune est atroce, et tout soleil amer.*
> *L'âcre amour m'a gonflé de torpeurs enivrantes.*
> *O! que ma quille éclate, O! que j'aille à la mer!*

To Rimbaud the wonderful of the moon-richened night is only atrocious and the probable of the glowing day only bitter.

All symbolism must start from actual facts and symbolize them, rather than combine them in merely logical patterns. Dante said of his own

21

symbolism that the first level is the literal meaning. A symbol that was not particularized in some way would be either nonsymbol or beyond symbol (God). For even the three mystic rings in the last Canto of the *Paradiso* are symbolic of the intuition of God. They do not equal God, though they transcend His mere effects of light and sound, however eternal and beautiful, in the *primum mobile*.

A question of degree is at issue. To cite two common symbols, the unicorn is further from natural fact than the fish; yet the unicorn is a synthesis of several natural animals. Compare angels and devils as symbols in medieval literature with Ibsen's wild-duck symbol, where presumably the latter would be a "combination of naturalism and symbolism." The angels and devils are imaginative syntheses of known physiological facts (light, blackness, physical force, lovely eyes, wings); the wild duck is a direct transformation of a physical fact to the symbolic level. Whole ducks exist in nature, as do the separate physical facts that are synthesized to create angel and devil symbols. How much the natural facts must change and combine does not determine the character of the fact in literature. There is either imaginative symbol or rationalist type, depending on the practice of the artist—assuming, as some do not, that art can be merely rationalist. The angel of Dante and the wild duck of Ibsen belong in the same class as symbols; but the wild duck is as far removed from a barnyard duck of Zola as is the angel.

There is no such thing as "naturalism and symbolism combined" in the foregoing sense of the terms, though symbolism can include naturalism in transcending it. Allegory is another matter. As John Finley points out, allegory is the literary method of the aesthetic rationalist; it is generally embodied as a physical representation of a *concept* by one who thinks probably and conceptually. Mr. Worldly Wiseman is rationalist, allegorical; Dante's angel, whatever Dante may have said rationally about him, is symbolic.

Joyce, then, does not achieve what has been credited to him, a "combination of naturalism and symbolism," not even outside the terminology of our system, although Dostoievsky or Shakespeare might. His writing is not symbolistic, but fourth-dimensional allegory. In *Ulysses,* family patterns, father-son, Bloom-Stephen, art-science, the events of the *Odyssey,* the times of day, the geography of Dublin, significant human events (birth, death, adultery, marriage, job) are analogically juxtaposed against one another, but allegorically and rationalistically. It is significant that both Joyce's great books are probable, social, mannered (*Finnegans Wake* will be discussed later in connection with comedy and the probable). To a conceptualist, this criticism of Joyce will appear a quibble. To one who understands symbolism (which Joyce half believed in, but was unable to achieve), it is the basic question to ask about the *attitude* of his art—scope being wholly, and depth partly another matter.

NOVELISTS OF THE PROBABLE AND THE WONDERFUL

It was said above that a thinker's view of predictability in life can focus his whole philosophy, as with the probable Mill or the nonprobable Kierkegaard. If this is so with philosophers, who write conceptually, it is all the more so with artists, whose work, since it deals in concrete facts (probable–wonderful), only secondarily focuses them into conceptualists or symbolists (reason–imagination). Lubbock notes two classes of novelists, one including Tolstoy and Flaubert; the other, Dostoievsky and Stendhal. Tolstoy writes of man's progress from birth to death in the gradual change of probable social life. In his work types move through life by predictable norms in a predictable society. In Flaubert also the focus is the probable and the predictable. Emma Bovary searches for the wonderful in the physical symbols of *social* distinction (the dinner party, the purchase of expensive clothes and furniture), in love affairs, in romantic novels. But, like the jaded Don Juan who seduces her, and who sizes her up (for she is predictable), she comes face to face with the probable. The great normal life course, childhood through death, holds her fast (symbolized by her giving birth to a child)—as do also the great norms of social experience, marriage and bourgeois life. When she seeks to escape these norms, which cannot be abandoned without the profoundest repercussions, she meets desertion by her lover and the disgrace of her husband's bankruptcy. Her financial ambition (the search for abnormal social position, not for money) forces her mediocre (normal)

23

husband to amputate the leg of the town clubfoot because he bungles a sensational cure. And because of her love affairs, her family is dissolved and her daughter is condemned to life as a factory worker. When one man, seeking pleasurable experience and not profound wisdom, leaves the groove of the probable, he disturbs for evil the whole society, especially in its smallest unit, the family. When the fathers have eaten sour grapes, the children's teeth are set on edge.

How different the world of *War and Peace* and *Madame Bovary* from the world of *The Idiot, The Red and the Black, The Castle!* Prince Myshkin, Julien Sorel, K, move through the night of individual discovery, each to the strange port of his own nature. Family, society, rational norms, predictability, count for little in these books. They are peopled with the unique souls of individuals, each of whom is alone in a universe where what happens is always unforeseen. General Epanchin's family, or the family of K's self-appointed messenger, are not probable, social families at all, like those in Tolstoy, even though they comprise groups whose members are bound to one another by ties of personality. We can predict what will happen to Emma within two or three possibilities. But who, seeing the clever, dreamy Julien Sorel installed as tutor in the provincial village (note the individuality, lack of familial meaning, of such a job) would ever wildly imagine his bloody head clutched at the end of the book by his young wife, the Parisian princess, raptly invoking her three-centuries-dead ancestor, Boniface de la Mole! While reading Stendhal, Kafka, and Dostoievsky, we are continually surprised. It is not the surprise of fanciful titillation, as in a Gothic novel or a detective story, but the surprise of symbolic discovery. In them we learn great truths about our own souls, while in Tolstoy and Flaubert we see our position in society more clearly. In Kafka we wince at our sins, in Flaubert at our *faux pas.*

Kafka reads Kierkegaard; Stendhal is a romanticist (there is symbolic meaning in his many changes of place and his numbers of pseudonyms). They are novelists of the wonderful, probers by imagination of the individual soul. The others are probable, rationalist, thinkers in social terms. Even when he becomes religious, Tolstoy remains a rationalist.

24

He cannot explore the problem of the wonderful in any but rationalist terms, which is why his moral choices seem so clumsy and why *Resurrection* reads as *Crime and Punishment* would if J. S. Mill had written it. For him, Anna Karenina is lost. For Dostoievsky, she would be a sinner whose mind had been deepened by evil.

Not always does an artist find himself young. The wonderful Strindberg and Eliot groped their way through the naturalism and rationalism they sprang from towards the wonderful religion most akin to their own souls.

NOVELISTS OF THE WONDERFUL-IN-PROBABLE · HENRY JAMES AND PROUST

In the Museum of Modern Art in New York hangs a picture of a huge tropical snake (the wonderful, death) creeping down the staircase of a normal wealthy home (the probable). Those who live in the tight norms of the probable see the darkness of the wonderful, sometimes on the threshold of every probable act. Of such stamp were Henry James and Proust, whose elaborate rehearsals of manners and sensations, in the tension of their probability, contain the wonderful, the snake on the staircase. The vague but constant anxiety as we read their books and the feeling of metaphysical awe which the totality of their work imparts, is evidence of this. In the tension of the long sentences of Proust, which seem so languid and sleepy—like a snake—and in the mannered subtlety of James' technique, lies the poised potential, the never-striking sting of death.

TOTEM AND TABOO

The world of totem is that of family, social connections, tribe. It is the probable around which the savage huddles to ward off the dark improbable, the brutal attack of a mana-filled nature which is always keen to catch him unawares. Totem is the law of success, of social action, of group achievement.

In antinomic tension to probable totem is wonderful taboo, the area of which is dark individual desire, lonely man in the hostile universe. All that was nonprobable or antisocial, from incest to the king, was taboo. The tribe took the totem along on the hunt, a group activity. The family tree in both the modern and literal senses was a totem; it determined whom one could and could not marry to found a normal family. But taboo channeled the action of the individual in key ego-friction areas— relations with women and with social superiors, particularly the king. The civilized ambiguity of Hamlet's search for truth/flight from reality is paralleled by the savage ambiguity of the Latin *sacer,* meaning both "holy" and "untouchable," nonprobable symbolically in both directions at once (in symbol the rational opposites unite into the wonderful). Frazer notes that the first kings of the Latin tribe were strangers. He who is taboo (nonprobable) in social distinction must also be nonprobable, a stranger, to the tribe. The Odysseus-Nausicaa story began as the folk motif of the local princess marrying the strange prince. It is the primitive equivalent of Julien Sorel's and the princess's fascination for the nonprobable in each other, the search of man actively and woman passively for the wonderful. Of similar cloth are all stories of the strange prince's arrival in the homeland court, from Beowulf at Hrothgar's meadhall to Joseph in Egypt.

SEX AND DEATH

The life of the herd gives pleasure to social man. He is driven by the desire for reproduction towards continuance of the society. It has often been observed that the sex urge is an impersonal (therefore social and probable) drive. It seeks merely to keep the race going, the type alive. In performance and in purpose, sex is a social act. The family is its basic unit in space and the generation in time, both of which units are probable in life and bound to the probability of the body's life cycle. To all views of life as probable sex is basic, from the primitive totem and fertility rites to all forms of comedy, the subjects of which are family, the difference between generations, types, the problems of sex, manners, and social action.

26

We desire to preserve our individual souls as well as to reproduce. The soul against pain, time, and death—this is the theme of the wonderful, the individual, the area of self-preservation and taboo. All intuitional thought, all human experience with the wonderful, has tragedy as its subject—the individual in the face of misfortune or death.

EDMUND BURKE'S "ON THE SUBLIME AND BEAUTIFUL"

Croce delivered what he thought was the *coup de grâce* to the term "sublime" in aesthetics, and it has been fashionable to ignore works on it, particularly when many men in our century are enchanted with the measuring rod of semantics and, in effect, consider all symbol-cluster terms meaningless. This has happened in face of the fact that much of such writing is profound aesthetics, not least Longinus' "On the Sublime" (a correct translation of the Greek *hypsos,* since both the English and the Greek words connote elevation and divinity). In particular, Edmund Burke has taken a beating at the hands of more than one shallow critic. Theories have been attributed to him—size as an aesthetic criterion, for example—which no man in his senses would hold.

To Burke, the sublime was individual, treated of death and terror, focused on pain, was linked with the instinct of self-preservation. Whence the qualities of the sublime in art were Privation (vacuity, darkness, solitude, silence), Vastness, Infinity, Difficulty, Magnificence, Unevenness, Roughness (as a shaggy cliff). Grief was its emotion and mountains were its natural symbol.

The beautiful treated of sex and joy, focused on pleasure, was social and linked with the instinct of reproduction. Its qualities were proportion, smallness, smoothness, delicacy, clearness and brightness, elegance, ease. Its emotion was delight and its symbol the lovely woman.

In terms of our system, the sublime is wonderful, about death; the beautiful is probable, about sex. This is an oversimplification, as are many of the foregoing suggestions. No symbol ever completely equals any other symbol.

27

The probable and the wonderful are antinomic symbols, forming a duality of which each member is dependent on and implies the other, as day does night; man, woman; spring, fall. The following facets of them have been discussed:

Probable	*Wonderful*
Social	Individual
Society	Artist
Politician (rationalist of pure action)	Searcher (mystic, artist, saint)
Reason (empirical, deductive, inductive)	Imagination
View of the wonderful as *a priori* thought	View of the probable as music of the spheres
Manners	Ethics
Mean (Aristotle)	Extreme (Christianity)
Predictability	Nonpredictability
Concept	Symbol
Classic　　　—Romantic—	Symbolic
Naturalism	Symbolism
Totem	Taboo
Sex	Death
Burke's Beautiful	Burke's Sublime

In the light of this duality, there are two basic ways of regarding life; in art this is the great generic duality, comedy versus tragedy.

THE NATURE OF COMEDY AND TRAGEDY

Qui sent, pleurt; qui pense, rit.
Le rire dans la rue; les pleurs à la maison.

—TWO FRENCH PROVERBS

Tragedy and comedy are symbolic attitudes. In them the contrasts are infinitely complex and the meaning of a single fact has infinite extension. Comedy is so rich and various that it is trivial to classify it descriptively as Aristotle, Freud, and Bergson do. The point is to probe its depths, not to chop it into portions. We remember Freud's theory of wit as the dispelling of hostility by cathexis, not his classes of jest, displacement, substitution; Bergson's theory of comedy as machine, not his "comedy of forms," or "comedy of movements."

Let the reader turn back to the table at the end of the preceding chapter. He will find many topics on the "probable" side—for example, manners, sex, naturalism—which suggest comedy; and on the "wonderful" side, many which suggest tragedy—for example, death, ethics, taboo. One way to probe the comedy–tragedy antinomy would be to run through in their order the less obviously comic–tragic members of the probable–wonderful table. But for reasons which will become clear by the end of this chapter, the subject has shifted ground, and the headings below will overlap only obliquely with those above.

WONDERFUL AS PROBABLE · PARADOX AND SYMBOL

As the individual makes his voyage of soul through the wonderful in life, he is guided by the insight of good and evil. Tragedy is the drama of this voyage and *ethics* the code which clarifies what in an action is sin and what salvation. In tragedy the usual symbol for the wonderful is its extreme instance for man—death. Death may be incurred by a voyage too far into the wonderful: by madness, as in Sophocles' *Ajax;* by search for superhuman knowledge, as with Dante's Ulysses in the twenty-sixth canto of the *Inferno;* by a too individualistic hedonism in the face of social demands, as with Shakespeare's Antony.

Suffering, as well as death, can symbolize the wonderful in tragedy. Job, Oedipus the King, Prometheus, do not die. Occasionally the protagonist may emerge from the dark storms of suffering into the calm of virtue (not innocence), as in Sophocles' *Philoctetes,* or *Oedipus at Colonnus.* Or he can continue infinitely to deepen, like most of the tragic characters in Dostoievsky. Not the outcome of the action, but its focus in terms of probable and wonderful, determines whether a play is comedy or tragedy. *Philoctetes* and *The Tempest* are both profound, and both have a happy ending; one is tragedy, the other comedy.

Tragedy's subject is wonderful-as-probable: man, death, tribulations of the soul. In the action of the individual, its ethics presents on the conceptual level the pattern of paradox: the disease/health of the searcher, the prosperity/adversity of the saint, the good/evil, altruism/egotism, pride/modesty of man's search for God. Especially in "classical" tragedians, such as Sophocles and Racine, the antithesis of paradox is elaborated over and over, and back again into itself. Blacks merge with whites; whites become blacks, and the motives of the protagonist are always antithetically ambiguous. Oedipus is king/polluted pariah; he hides/reveals his guilt, which is fated/willed; he is infinitely wise/utterly ignorant; he sees/is blind, whereas Tiresias is blind/sees. At the end of the play he is made whole by a great wound. Pity–terror, the tragic spectator's emotion according to Aristotle, holds the ambiguity of the religious man's motivation; it might be transposed as "altruistic–egotistic sorrow." The paradox of Kierkegaard or Heraclitus says, not "Man cannot know" (though partly that), but "Man must probe deeper, into the level of symbolic truth, for his ethics to gain religious meaning."

Tragedy, as John Finley points out, is born after the advent of conceptualism; and conceptualism deepens tragedy by ordering it within the tensions of a logical pattern. Yet tragedy is not allegory, concepts clothed in metaphor. It is symbol; the probable concepts of paradox are stretched tight over the symbolic wonderful. The penultimate stage of the soul's journey is always ambiguous; in the ultimate state, light–darkness, guilt–innocence, free will–fate, all resolve themselves into the pure light of symbol. The elaborate paradoxes of *Oedipus Rex* melt into symbolic glow in *Oedipus at Colonnus,* when the soul, purified and on the threshold of death, finds its ultimate destination.

Instead of using paradox, a tragedian may express himself directly in antinomic symbols. The supreme example of this is *Antony and Cleopatra,* with its antinomies (besides the title itself) of sea–land, war–peace, battle–sex, Rome–Egypt, city–Nile, duty–pleasure, empire–man. But even when the surface pattern is the antithesis of paradox, tragedy's religious meaning is always symbolic. Usually nothing appears more conceptual than the ethics of religious thought and tragedy. Actually, nothing is less so.

When the tragedian himself does not understand this, his tragedy suffers in depth. Euripides thought he was a conceptual thinker, and his plays are the worse for every line of rationalistic talk. He is redeemed only by the destructive instincts of the wonderful—cruel Aphrodite, the unconcerned chastity of Artemis in the *Hippolytus,* war in the *Trojan Women.* As Sophocles found harmony in the symbol of Apollo, so Euripides realized himself most fully in the *Bacchae* with the destructive Dionysus.

Dreaming Apollo and drunken Dionysus are polar in the world of the wonderful. Apollo is the wonderful-as-probable—god of the glowing, probable day, of success, medicine, and music. He guides the state and wards off the wonderful destroyers, the Furies. Through him come success, harmony, and light. He is the redeemer in social meaning of the visionary prophet. Dionysus is the god of wonderful failure, the dark instincts of cruel spring; in that season he leads his drunken band of individuals by moonlight to the leafy mountains for a destructive orgy of sex, dancing, and slaughter—drinking the wine of rivers and the milk of lionesses, slaying lions and bulls. He serves both as the patron god of comedy and as the leader of seekers for the wonderful who purge in themselves its destruction.

The insight of Nietzsche has traced the antinomy of Apollo and Dionysus through Greek culture, endowing their polarity with universal validity. Euripides understood only Dionysus; to him Apollo was a hypocritical god who got his female devotee with child *(Ion).*

MANNERS–ETHICS

Social man experiences and predicts the norms of life. His goal is not to save his soul but to avoid pain and enjoy pleasure. He strives for comfort by following the mean and adapting himself as closely as possible to the

33

social norm. Whether lawyer, husband, businessman, or diplomat, he proceeds by what Henderson (a self-styled follower of Pareto) calls the case system—the experiencing of norms as they emerge in continued pure action and the treatment of recurring cases according to these norms. Social thought and its art form, comedy, considers not the *extreme* value of good and evil, but the pure-action *mean* of best policy. In the thought of Machiavelli, this is the basis of all action between governments; and Machiavelli holds a high position in Italian literary history as a comic writer.

An expanding imperialist society—fifth-century Athens, seventeenth-century France, nineteenth-century Britain, America today—will always produce increasing numbers of pure-action diplomats and, in their wake, great comic poets—Aristophanes, Molière, W. S. Gilbert, Chaplin. In her rapid transition from country town to empire, Athens shows this markedly in such social phenomena as the Sophists, who plotted, like the social psychologists in our own expanding empire, the rationales of propaganda and the handling of men in masses. In the plays of Sophocles, Creon is the diplomat whose probable, social rationales of policy making contrast and clash with the wonderful, tragic, religious thought of Oedipus and his daughter Antigone. The crafty burgher Odysseus of Homer becomes the pure-action diplomat of Sophocles' *Philoctetes*.

The unit in tragedy, as in novels of the wonderful, is man alone; in comedy, the family. In tragedy, sex is always the love affair, the experience of the soul. Marriage, the probable in sex, is always distant, either approached in courtship, as in Corneille's *Cid,* or drawing constantly away and never achieved, as often in the novels of Dostoievsky. The love affair can be temptation (*Phèdre*) or a hindrance to social duty (*Bérénice*). As de Rougemont interprets it, the love of the Tristram myth masks supreme egotism/supreme death-wish; the individual's search for the wonderful in the most probable of man's social activities is really the search for death. Love–death is a profound symbol for man. It occurs so frequently in tragic opera as to be almost a convention of the form. Poe, the romantic follower of the wonderful, thought that love–death was the greatest theme of imaginative literature.

34

In comedy the member of the old generation, father or mother of the girl, may often threaten a lover with death. But the destructive force is always social—the family or its agents—and sex always succeeds in spite of opposition. Sex in comedy is either the physical act, as in early comic fertility rituals, Aristophanes, modern burlesque, or the social norm of marriage and the family. Comedy mocks romantic love as an abnormal hoax (Sheridan and Gilbert) or considers it the prelude to marriage. The sexual abnormalities which are ludicrous to probable comedy are not the sin of love–death, but cuckoldry, the denial of the marriage norm, and homosexuality, the denial of normal instinct. Molière and Shakespeare are obsessed with the one, Aristophanes with the other. Novelists of the probable like Zola and James T. Farrell are also much concerned with them.

Tragedy's subjects are the wonderful, sin, and death; comedy's the probable, politics, and sex. Tragedy is sublime in Burke's sense, and comedy beautiful. In comedy, politics and sex can be treated separately—politics as in the satires of Swift and Samuel Butler, the *Wasps* and *Knights* of Aristophanes; sex as in Semonides' "Castigation of Women," the *Thesmophoriazusae,* most plays of Molière; or they may be combined, as in the comedy-of-manners genre, the *Lysistrata* and *Ecclesiazusae;* or placed side by side as facets of social life, as in the satires of Juvenal and Swift; or interwoven as in most of Gilbert's plays, the *Odyssey*—for example, the relation between Odysseus' impression on Nausicaa and his status in Phaeacia—*Measure for Measure,* and *The Tempest.*

The soul of man is saved through avoiding evil and performing good, through *ethics.* Social man, to incur least shock from society and to reap most profit from business, politics, and sex, employs *manners,* the pure-action norms of social experience.

INDIVIDUAL–MEMBER OF A GENERATION

In tragedy the age of the protagonist is an incidental part of the symbol. The aged Lear, the young Hamlet, the middle-aged Othello, are all struggling souls before time, though the poet may stress the time of life more in some cases than others—for example, middle age in

35

Antony and Cleopatra. As in novels of the wonderful, the soul is alone in time, and its age has meaning only for the individual. Man, the wonderful individual as supreme probable, is central to tragedy. Family, the norm in space, and generation, the norm in time, are reflected only obliquely in the wonderful soul.

In comedy social man's position is determined by his relation to generation and to family; it is important whether he is bachelor or paterfamilias, son, husband, or father. In the primitive fertility rituals the old man tries to slay the young, and fails; this rudimentary pattern is reflected in the antiphonal debate for sexual possession of the young man between the young woman and the old near the end of Aristophanes' *Ecclesiazusae,* in the eternal springing back to life in the Punch and Judy show, in the debate of Alcuin's poem between young Spring and old Winter as to whether the cuckoo shall come and bring the flowers and the sun. The ideas of the father versus the ideas of the son, the older generation versus the younger generation, are at the core of the family in comedy from Aristophanes to *Finnegans Wake*: Strepsiades versus Pheidippides in the *Clouds,* Philocleon versus Bdelycleon in the *Wasps,* the fathers and their lost sons in Plautus and Terence, the middle-aged suitor versus the young lover in Molière and Gilbert and Sullivan, the gradations of age in *The Way of All Flesh,* the Falstaff–Mistress Page middle-aged plot versus the Anne Page–Fenton young-love plot in *The Merry Wives of Windsor,* father's and son's romances in *The Rivals,* in the *Knight of the Burning Pestle,* the generations in the probable *Cherry Orchard* and *War and Peace,* Anna Livia Plurabelle versus her daughter and HCE versus his sons in *Finnegans Wake* and so on.

Comedy represents ideas not as eternal truths but as the probable clothing of a specific time of life. The radical younger generation becomes conservative as it grows older. The idealistic poet of twenty-five will be a pragmatic man of action by forty, unless he is a fool, like Ricky Ticky Tavy, the shallow poet in *Man and Superman.* The young romantic lover becomes the prosaic middle-aged husband. What is normal for one generation is abnormal for another. Liberalism is expected for the young Pheidippides, but abnormal and ridiculous in the middle-aged Socrates. Gil-

36

bert presents in many characters the slightly ridiculous figure of the middle-aged woman who plays the romantic lover, like Buttercup in *H.M.S. Pinafore,* and Katisha in *The Mikado.* When the Rapturous Maidens at the beginning of *Patience* sing:

> *Twenty love-sick maidens we,*
> *Love-sick all against our will.*
> *Twenty years hence we shall be*
> *Twenty love-sick maidens still.*
> *Twenty love-sick maidens we,*
> *And we die for love of thee . . .*

this is humorous, because the audience assumes, as is probable, that they will be matrons and middle-aged mothers "twenty years hence," not struck with passions that in comedy belong only to young girlhood. They prove this by marrying not Bunthorne the poet but the army officers who have consistently been courting them. If Isolde or Cleopatra were to sing something like this, it would not be funny at all.

In tragedy man is a soul before God; his history is the history of his sins and good acts. In comedy social man is a youth, a middle-aged father, or an old grandfather. All activities are normal for a certain age only. If you try to indulge in what is improbable for your age, you yourself become improbable and ridiculous. Shaw's dictum, "Old age forgives itself everything and is forgiven nothing; youth forgives itself nothing and is forgiven everything," might be expanded: "Members of the old generation, by long normal experience in life, have come to the conclusion that the brief span of life should be spent in pleasure. But old people are abnormal in society; society as a whole demands adherence to the norms, especially from those with the greatest experience in forming norms. Only those who are fledglings in experience will be forgiven their hedonism; they should have a normal generation-period, while young, of sowing wild oats, narrowing their experience into norms, before they settle down into the rut of the probable. But it seems that the younger generation, since it has had little experience of norms, indulges in nonprobable, religious, liberal political speculation. Youth most castigates itself for sins

37

by the standards of wonderful religion at the time when probable society is most willing to forgive its foibles by the standards of probable folk wisdom." Shaw's gnomic aphorism is a perfect summation of the comic view of man as a member of a generation and a family.

GOOD–EVIL VERSUS CONFORMITY–EXPULSION

The basic concern of ethics is saving the soul of individual man, who is constantly making choices between good and evil in the world To tragedy, extreme ethics implies extreme social position, an abnormal protagonist. Oedipus as holy wanderer and Lear as suffering outcast are greater and deeper souls than either was as king. The vision of the tragic hero is deepened not only when he becomes outcast, but because he bcomes outcast. The higher the artist climbs in thought, the farther the saint proceeds in virtue, the more abnormal these searchers become. Tragedy, from the *Prometheus* of Aeschylus to the *Idiot* of Dostoievsky, traces the causal connection between the abnormal search of the tragic hero and his suffering at the hands of normal society. Occasionally society may enshrine him in the glow of its own hallowed nonprobability, the aristocracy of the accepted priesthood; more often it turns him from the social body as outcast, mendicant, or prisoner. As the primitive rite of sexual license for fertility stands in the shadow behind comedy, so the rite of the hanged god, the perfect sacrifice, stands behind tragedy. When Apollo gave Cassandra the gift of prophecy, he gave her also the necessity that she be misunderstood; each implied the other. In the deepest sense the seer is prophetic; not that he sees specific events before they occur, but that he lives in the spirit of the future. Nonprobable in the present, he speaks forth what will have meaning in the normal future embodiment of the civilization. Normal society harrowed the souls of the Hebrew prophets, crucified the Son of God, and continued to martyrize His saints long after His religion had, in its outward forms, become official. That the Second Person of the Trinity's tragic–triumphant crucifixion followed the age-old racial norms of the hanged god, only centralizes its meaning. If it had been otherwise, we might doubt more, not less, its validity.

Usually tragedy proceeds by contrasts, beginning with a hero, played by a handsome actor, who is the flower of normal social success. Comedy likewise is a contrast, between the ugly, buffoonish clown who is the central figure, and the norms he implies by violating them. Part of the clown's meaning is, "those who indulge to excess their normal appetites for sex, eating, beating their friends, saying what they please, will be expelled from the normal society for their nonconformity to manners." We laugh, and society draws together into the conformity of its norm, expelling the abnormal individualist. It is the rich man's silk hat knocked off with a snowball that causes laughter. The nonprobable power of wealth is transformed into the impotence of the nonprobable clown. The individualist may be equally a drunkard, a satyr, an aristocrat, a saint, or an artist; in any case, nonsocial abnormality is expelled from society by laughter. In this sense laughter is superiority, though always the superiority of a group which follows the mean over the abnormal individual whose excess it constrains.

The most subtle abnormal individual in society is the searcher and the thinker, wherefore his expulsion from the group is one of comedy's most common topics. Comedy represents his search as the perversion of probable activities. Useless speculation (abnormal failure) contrasts with pure-action knowledge; liberal (therefore impracticable) schemes with practical politics; romantic love with marital sex. In comedy even the nonprobable person's actions remain political and sexual.

The normal and the probable of comedy is always rationalist; but the distinction should be made between objective rationalism, which is probability, and the intellectual rationalist thinker, who is nonprobable in society. The normal man does not govern his life by the abstractions of ethics but by the pure-action norms of manners. Never does he turn inward to consider self-consciously his own action; he merely dreams himself into existence. He avoids pain in society, not blots on the soul. From the comic point of view, reason is always the rationalization of egotistic selfishness, as in this passage from *Iolanthe*:

> Lord Chancellor: Victory! Victory! Success has crowned my efforts, and I may consider myself engaged to Phyllis! At first I wouldn't hear of it—it was out of the question [because he is her guardian].

But I took heart. I pointed out to myself that I was no stranger to myself; that, in point of fact, I had been personally acquainted with myself for some years. This had its effect. I admitted that I watched my professional advancement with considerable interest, and I handsomely added that I yielded to no one in admiration for my private and professional virtues. This was a great point gained. I then endeavoured to work upon my feelings. Conceive my joy when I distinctly perceived a tear glistening in my own eye! Eventually, after a severe struggle with myself, I reluctantly—most reluctantly—consented.

All intellectuals are abnormal in society, and as such they are laughed out of the group in comedy, usually by exposing the selfish half of the paradox of their motivation: the theoreticians who violate probability with their schemes in Swift; Thwackum and Square in *Tom Jones;* Socrates in the *Clouds;* Bunthorne the poet in *Patience,* who confesses he is only trying to attract attention; the spiritual fairies in *Iolanthe,* who significantly belong to no generation. From the point of view of probable comedy, all religious men who try to become abnormally virtuous end as Tartuffes. In tragedy those who search to purify their souls are saved, though they die in the attempt. *Wer immer strebend sich bemüht, den können wir erlösen.*

As the social group becomes normal by expelling the abnormal individual in comedy, so the individual by wit adjusts himself to society. Freud shows that wit, a humorous sally among individuals in a small social group, hides the desire for the release of social tension. Through wit the individual expels from himself hostility, aggression, inferiority, all antisocial feelings, or identifies himself with the rest of the group by ridiculing some other person; in both cases the witty person adjusts to society by agreeing with it in the concept behind the joke. This is why the actor on the comic stage can laugh, though he is being expelled; he recognizes the abnormality of his norm in society and is happy therein. In comedy, everybody is happy in his social station.

Freud points out the similarity between the mechanisms underlying both wit and the dream. But wit, by a quick discharge of energy, achieves social success, whereas the dream is individual, the purging of the inner mind:

> The dream is a perfectly asocial psychic product . . . . it can only exist in disguised form; Wit, on the other hand, is the most social of all those psychic functions whose aim is to gain pleasure. No matter how concealed, the dream is still a wish, while wit is a developed play. The dream serves preponderantly to guard against pain, while wit serves to acquire pleasure.

Economy, the law of least possible action (the norm in scientific terms), always gives pleasure. Often diplomatic action can be achieved most economically by humor. Brill's example, quoted by Freud, well demonstrates this:

> Wendell Phillips . . . was on one occasion lecturing in Ohio, and while on a railroad journey . . . met in the car a number of clergymen. . . . One of the ministers . . . asked him, "Are you Mr. Phillips?" "I am, sir." "Are you trying to free the niggers?" "Yes, sir; I am an abolitionist." "Well, why do you preach your doctrines up here? Why don't you go over into Kentucky?" "Excuse me, are you a preacher?" "I am, sir." "Are you trying to save souls from hell?" "Yes, sir, that's my business." "Well, why don't you go there?"

This is funny because it refocuses the surprise climax, "why don't you go there?" into the predictable and probable. It also suffuses Mr. Phillips and the other clergymen with a glow of humorous joy, because it unites the group and saves it the pain of perhaps an hour's argument; the humorous remark at that point in the conversation achieved economically what could only have been done otherwise by a long serious discourse.

FAILURE–SUCCESS

The symbolic soul, which always sees the nonpredictable wonderful in the world outside and its own sinful guilt within, stands sorrowfully in contemplation, fails in earthly pursuits, dies. The rational social mind, seeing that most social activities are probable and predictable, joyously enters pure action, succeeds, prospers, and procreates. In tragedy man always dies and fails on earth; he always lives and succeeds in comedy. It is proverbial that you cannot kill the comic hero. In the old rituals, a character stood by ready to revive him. Odysseus' crew may be winnowed like sheds in a tornado, but never Odysseus himself. Whirlpools, giants, monsters, sorceresses, even the god Poseidon, cannot down his plucky optimism and his social adroitness. Nature is the greatest healer; the rationalist doctor should take his black arts and vanish: this is the meaning of *Le Malade Imaginaire,* with its contrast between the healthy, youthful life of the natural shepherds in the entr'acte ballets, and the stuffy apartments of Argan, with their beds, medicaments, and bandages. But, if Argan persists in priming nature, he will marry his daughter to a doctor; better still, become a doctor himself. In the mumbo jumbo and revel dance of the last scene, the unmasking of the arcana of medicine seems in no way to make Argan less happy about the possibilities of his own cure. Comedy shouts, "Only in the norms of society is there health." And it is backed up by the rationalistic analysis of the social psychologist. But tragedy, resigning itself to failure on this earth, sighs back, "Ah, but those who are low in the cities of earth may become high in the city of God." And it is redeemed by the vision of the artist and the ecstasy of the saint.

TRAGEDY AND COMEDY AS ART FORM AND STAGE CONVENTION

The plays of Aeschylus were "slices from the banquet of Homer." The plot of every extant classical tragedy but the *Persians* was a motif widespread in oral and written tradition. Shakespeare got his plots almost exclusively from his readings in romance and history. There is nearly always a direct source to be traced for the tragic plot.

On the other hand, the comic playwright, from Aristophanes to Shaw, invents his plots. Their basic pattern may be traced in folk ritual, but only infrequently can a direct source be found. Comic plots are the new, the nonprobable. Society views them, adjusts them to the probable, and laughs in the process, because success is achieved, the unpredictable has been made predictable, the New Year is like the old.

The plot of tragedy is probable, and the protagonist a normal and successful aristocrat. Gradually the individuality of his soul unfolds, the predictable becomes unpredictable, the wonderful is revealed beneath the superficial pattern of the probable, and the audience weeps in recognition of the mystery and tragedy of life. In comedy, almost never does a character represent the norm, which laughs at him and expels him as he implies it by his abnormality. Both comedy and tragedy, in the pattern of plot and character, proceed by the tension of contrast. Comedy says, "Even in the abnormal and the unpredictable do norms and predictability emerge." For the comic abnormal hero is always a type—country bumpkin, boaster, ironist, misanthrope, miser, middle-aged cuckold, young lover, foreigner. They are all funny because their abnormality implies and strengthens the norm, because even they are typical norms of abnormality.

The comic plot is always full of surprises; the situations always detour from the probabilities we expect. Kant saw all laughter as "an affection arising from a strained expectation being suddenly reduced to nothing." The very patterns of the torrent of jokes in a comic play are typed as "against expectation," which Aristotle explained as the cause of tickling and one of the most prevalent types of humor (for example, "son of a pitchmeoutofasecondstorywindow"). In popular humor whole poems, usually with sexual innuendos, are composed on this pattern. Society laughs, not only because it is able to predict its surprise but, in the case of the sexual innuendo, because it perceives the norm of the mores deflecting the explicit sexual reference into the harmless surprise. We are continually delighted that the wit can plunge headlong against the mores at every turn and dodge aside just in time with an unexpected nonsexual word. We laugh at him, at ourselves, even at the mores; but the norms remain, and are preserved for society by the wit which pleasurably releases the tension. Freud says the dirty joke originates as an oblique approach to seduction; certainly, without reference to psychological theories, the sexual license of a comic play implies the saturnalian license of action; in most rituals of fertility the comic play occurs at the same time as the Saturnalia.

Often the comic hero voyages toward the new, as in the voyages of

43

Odysseus over the seas, the travels of Don Quixote, the folk migrations in *Finnegans Wake,* the entrance into new social modes in *Les Femmes Savantes* and *Le Bourgeois Gentilhomme*. But the wonder of these new areas always emerges in experience as the probability of the old. Don Juan Tenerie, *alter ego* of John Tanner, in the dream scene of *Man and Superman,* finds that the norms of experience in Don Juan's time are very like those in his own. When Peisthetairos and Euelpides in the *Birds* of Aristophanes leave the probabilities of Athenian politics to found a city for the wonderful birds, they find that the political problems of the new city striate themselves into the very patterns they abandoned in old Athens. Odysseus finds politics and sexual life in Phaeacia much the same as in Ithaca, and Alice in *Wonder*land meets situations understandable in terms of the norms of life on this earth. Where comedy says, "even in the nonprobable does the predictable take place," tragedy says, "even in the probable, the wonderful is manifest."

The basic convention of the stage is objective perspective; the audience and the actors stand in a third-personal, not the normal second-personal, relationship to one another. In tragedy the players on the stage are as objective to the spectators as if they were in a book. But comedy always violates this convention; the actor reaches out of the frame of objectivity and addresses the audience second-personally; and the spectators all laugh, affirming the norm of the objectivity convention, successfully apprehending that the violation is abnormal, and typing it into the predictability of abnormality shortly after it has occurred unpredictably. Parody of the conventions of the stage, of other dramas, of clichés, of jokes and poetry— all these are abundant and natural in comedy, which jauntily laughs at all art, including itself. Aristophanes, W. S. Gilbert, Molière, and Joyce refer constantly to their own works and to themselves. The modern major general can "whistle all the airs from that infernal nonsense, *Pinafore."* Aristophanes parodies Sophocles and Agathon, Megarian farce, Heracles as a stock character, and the choruses of Euripides; Gilbert, pre-Raphaelite poetry, Italian and Wagnerian opera, oracular pronouncements through music; Joyce, the processes of history, the clichés of popular fiction, even his own life history in the story of Jim the Penman (*Finnegans Wake*).

Irony in tragedy is the contrast between the spectator's knowledge and the character's ignorance. In comedy, irony is a second-personal joke between some of the characters and the audience; the butt of the joke can be either the abnormal character type or a member of the audience, as often in Aristophanes and in modern burlesque. Swift in *Gulliver's Travels* laughs second-personally with the reader at the abnormal speculators and their impractical schemes.

The statement in tragedy unheard by the rest of the actors is the soliloquy, addressed by the individual protagonist to his own soul. In comedy, it is the aside, addressed by one of the actors second-personally to the social group that constitutes the audience. Tragedy, by rigidly observing the stage convention, creates the illusion of reality; we are to take the play seriously and identify ourselves as individuals with the protagonist— whence our pity and terror. Comedy, violating the stage convention, says, "Ah, but this is only a play; these characters are abnormal; or if the license of their abnormality is our secret desire and these sins our foibles, they are to be ritually expelled by our social laughter, and can secretly be enjoyed in real life with impunity." Some thinkers, Feibleman and Shaw for example, do not understand this. They think that comedy, which laughs at the habits of society, is an instrument of social reform. The Russians are more perceptive; comedy is the only form of social criticism they permit.

The person relationship around a play is triangular—characters, author, reader-spectator. The popular mind identifies the author with his characters, expecting thereby to see a handsome and aristocratic tragedian, an ugly and buffoonish comic writer. The opposite is usually the case. Dan Chaucer was not the fat, rollicking funster of popular legend, but a suave courtier who made his way from bourgeois origins to the high offices of governmental service; further, he was an intellectual who held the mastery of several esoteric disciplines, including astrology and Latin literature; who translated superbly two of the masterpieces of medieval literature, the tragic *De Consolatione* of Boethius and the *Roman de la Rose*. Shakespeare was a shrewd man of business, Gilbert educated in law, Fielding a magistrate. Machiavelli wrote comedies, and it is well known that successful men in the world often have the capacity for wit; they are the ones

45

who know the probable of society, and have climbed into the laxness of aristocratic nonprobability.

A neurosis has driven the comic artist also out of the norm. For he is still goaded by the dark drive to create; the clown with a broken heart is always the writer of his own jokes. But neurosis for a comic artist is all inward; the outer mask is social competence. Thereby the artist learns the norms of the probable, which in his comedy he transcends in art and reaffirms in laughter. Even when he assumes the mask of pariah in his own comedies, he is not to be thought the abnormal social incompetent he portrays. Contrast the helplessness of Charlie Chaplin, comic actor, with the well-known social mastery of Charles Chaplin, director and lover.

SUPERHUMAN–SUBHUMAN

Aristotle says in the *Poetics* that tragedy and comedy represent men as better or worse than among us. In tragedy, the protagonist is always a great-souled hero, an aristocrat from the dim heroic past—Achilles, Prometheus, Siegfried, Parsifal, Roland; or a king, a chief of men—Lear, Hamlet, Othello, Agamemnon; or at least of noble status. He may actually achieve godhead, as the unknown stranger Dionysus in the *Bacchae* of Euripides; in the great Sanskrit epics, heroes are often avatars, gods in human form and flesh: Vishnu incarnated as Rama in the *Ramayana,* or Krishna in the *Mahabharata;* or direct descendents of the gods, like Karna, child of the sun, in the *Mahabharata.* The battle of the wonderful soul with its own guilt takes place in the cosmic and symbolic realm of good and evil. In *Paradise Lost* the scope rises and broadens to include God and good angels battling Satan and the bad angels for the soul of Adam, in the whole universe.

As tragedy shows the godlike in man, so comedy shows the bestial. Man as beast, as social animal, is predictable and probable. Basic to all comedy is beast fable, in its protean forms throughout the world—the Sanskrit *Hitopadesha* and *Panchatantra,* Aesop and La Fontaine, Uncle Remus, Archilochus and his fox-eagle tale, Semonides' comparison of women with beasts, the *Birds, Wasps, Frogs* of Aristophanes, the medieval *Ecbasis Captivi,* the noble horses in Swift, Reynard the Fox, frogs, snakes, and

46

beavers in Dante's *Inferno*, the beast masks in *Midsummer Night's Dream, The Merry Wives of Windsor,* and *Comus.*

As the tragedy of the hero's soul illumines individual religious truth, so the comedy of beast fable, like all comedy, presents social, probable wisdom, proverbs, rules of pure action. The beast fable is circumscribed within the area of gnomic, social wisdom.

The totem, which was probable, was always an animal. Man, insofar as he follows brute appetite and instinct, follows the rational, predictable norms of social action. When men are represented comically as beasts, we laugh because we know that inasmuch as they are bestial we can be successful by predicting them. We laugh also because we realize that beasts as characters in comedy are suprabestial; they represent the social ego-involvements of human beings. Therein we laugh joyously for our own social success. Surely, says beast fable in undertone, if man is suprabestial, there is nothing superhuman; all is predictable and probable; the area of man's activity is completely social.

The same surprising contrast comes when we see human beings acting like machines—making jerky motions, repeating the same phrase endlessly, exhibiting a rational pattern that is completely predictable. Bergson, in his theory of comedy as mechanism, meant "machine" in precisely the sense of "rational probable" in this essay. For he believed in the two levels of predictable, rational extensive manifold and unpredictable, suprarational intensive manifold. The contrast is between subman-as-machine and real man-as-supramechanical. Again, the surprise of subman is apprehended, categorized, and transformed into the nonsurprise of predictability. The social laughter perceives the essence of man as social man, and implicitly denies the individual soul of supraman. Tragedy reveals the soul of the individual hero; comedy represents the all-too-human under the rational subguise of beast or machine.

ARISTOCRAT–BOURGEOIS

Whether he performs a nonprobable social function as diplomat or officer, or has dried into effeteness through generations, the aristocrat lives the life of the wonderful individual. Not his the details of business, but only

47

the wonderful personal relationships of the nonprobable flower of society
—horses, athletics, romantic love, official religion. The protagonist in tragedy is an aristocrat. In one sense the glow of his harmonious happiness
transforms itself into the dark searchings of his wandering soul; yet in
another sense only the ease and individuality of his social position permit
the possibility of voyaging at all. Lear can run the gamut from king to
prophet; one of his subjects would simply go insane. There is a certain
leisure and luxury about any artist, however poor, that makes him hated
by his plebeian brethren. In the last war, it was mostly the Air Corps pilots
and naval officers who wrote poetry in service; the enlisted man was
locked so closely into the probability of a tight tribal society that his only
outlet was comedy—and in that he was abundantly fertile.

The bourgeois plebian is normal in society. Whereas the aristocrat nearly
always has love affairs—or numerous concubines like the Indian princes,
or a series of marriages and mistresses like Louis XIV and the present
movie colony, our American aristocracy—the bourgeois always marries.
He has not gained the freedom from the mores that money and a carefree
childhood bequeath. He is always the subject of comedy; even the gods in
comedy are bourgeois—Dionysus in the *Frogs,* Heracles in the *Birds,*
Hermes in the *Plutus.* Of the two classes that emerge in medieval French
literature, the aristocratic is definitely tragic (*Chansons de geste,* the
Romans, courtly love), the bourgeois comic (*Fabliaux,* the *Roman de
Renart, Les Quinze Joyes de Mariage*). In great comedy—Aristophanes,
Molière, Shakespeare—there is tension between the normative past as the
ideals of the aristocracy, and the norms of present life as the life of the
bourgeois.

SATIRE AND RATIONALISM

Satire springs from a ritual source like that of comedy, the fertility festival
of the full bowl (*lanx satura*); and satire, like comedy, is both probable
and rationalistic. Its subjects are always man in society, sex, and politics.
Whereas comedy laughs joyously over the norms of its contemporary
society, satire laughs sardonically at those norms; to satire the times are
out of joint. It sees the failure and corruption of the present as abnormal,

48

judged implicitly against a norm of success and health, in the past of a golden age or in the imagined future. To Juvenal, Rome is an extreme which future ages will look to as great excess from the mean:

> Nil erit ulterius quod nostris moribus addat
> Posteritas.

When Juvenal satirizes the corrupt woman, or Martial the avaricious undertaker, both assume a norm of honest woman and unmercenary undertaker. Dante, who castigates the corruption of Florence in his day, praises the norms of its practices in the day of his great-great-grandfather. An even bitterer satire, the reproach of womankind in Semonides, Hipponax, and the *Greek Anthology,* looks neither to the past nor to the future for noncorruption; but it rationalistically laughs in probable success because it can know woman and therefore predict her.

James Feibleman's book, *In Praise of Comedy,* represents comedy as satiric criticism of the present limited historical order and as campaign for the unlimited ideal logical order of the future. It is true that all comic drama is partly satire, from the savage tendentiousness of Aristophanes to the delicate ribbing of W. S. Gilbert and Samuel Butler. But basically comedy is approval, not disapproval, of present society; it is conservative, not liberal, however much the socialist Feibleman would like it to be. It expels the intellectual and his futuristic programs. If comedians like Shaw are liberal, to that degree they are noncomedians. The liberal element in Shaw's dramas is the noncomic element.

EMPIRICISM · DEDUCTION–INDUCTION · SYMBOLISM

Comic and tragic drama are both functions of symbolic thought. Since, as was pointed out in Chapter I, symbolic pure action and symbolic thought are identical, the two are fused in art, which is always symbolic. Yet in a deep sense comedy denies the existence of the symbol it uses and expels its own creator. Comedy presents empiricism plus rationalism (deductive-inductive), and denies symbolism (which it employs). The instinct of the comic poet has perceived this. Juvenal and Molière felt called on in their prefaces and Aristophanes in his choruses to plead for the seriousness of the function they were performing; they too, like the tragic artist, were on the defensive in society. And Molière thought it a strange occupation to *faire rire les honnêtes gens* (men of social position and wisdom).

Tragedy fuses empirical pure action and symbolic thought; whereby all action has its religious implications. It presents the rationalistic pattern of paradox, shows it to be self-contradictory in resolution, and thereby implies the third, symbolic level where the existence of good and evil is demanded by faith. Comedy, presenting pure action and symbol, reveals as true the rationalism of social norms; tragedy fuses pure action and symbol, and denies the rationalistic picture of ethics. Still, as the music of Bach and Byzantine mosaics use the *a priori* conceptual structure as symbol, so tragedy uses logical paradox as symbol. This may be expressed in a table:

	Comedy	*Tragedy*
Empiricism (pure action)	Presented	Fused with symbol
Rationalism (deductive-inductive)	Implicitly true	Used as symbol; shown as finally misrepresenting
Symbolism	Used, yet expelled	Fused with action

Tragedy and comedy, like life (of which they are living fruits) exist as infinite symbols; any symbolic ordering of them referentially entails their distortion. We have probed their meaning by focusing them into the following antinomies:

Tragedy	*Comedy*
Ethics	Manners
Individual man	Social man as the member of a family and generation
Wonderful-as-supreme-probable	Normal or abnormal type
History of the soul	Experience in social life

50

No distinction in generation	Position in generation as part of type
Death, good, evil	Politics, sex, search for the wonderful in probable terms (religion as selfishness; romantic love as ridiculous sex)
Good–evil	Conformity–expulsion
Ideas as absolutes	Ideas as property of members of a particular generation
Handsome actor	Ugly actor
Pariah artist	Diplomatic artist
Normal protagonist	Abnormal protagonist
Motif plot	Invented plot
Failure	Success
All in terms of soul	Denial of soul
Soliloquy	Aside
Adherence to third-personal stage convention	Second-personal flouting of third-personal convention
Superhuman	Subhuman (beast, machine)
Aristocrat	Bourgeois
Paradox	Contrast and assimilation of unexpected surprise to expected probable

The antinomic symbols summarized in the table at the end of Chapter I also apply.

ARISTOPHANES
SYMBOL IN TRIBE · CONCEPT IN EMPIRE

τὸ γὰρ δίκαιον οἶδε καὶ τρυγῳδία . . .

—ACHARNIANS

Athens in the flush of her last great naval victory, Arginusae (406 B.C.), was ripe for a discussion of art's relation to society, a more philosophical subject than that of most of her comedies, which dealt directly with the war.

In the *Frogs* Dionysus, the popularistic god of the comic-dramatic festival, judges in the underworld a contest between Aeschylus, the poet of tradition, and Euripides, the poet of modernism. Dionysus, who has sat in the god's chair at the comic festival since its institution by Pisistratus, is the ideal spectator, the very type of Athenian democratic man. He is represented throughout the play as a hedonistic plebeian whose easily titillated taste is as amoral as a passion for soup (to which he compares his liking for Euripides). Originally he departs for the underworld to bring the recently deceased Euripides back to earth. He has been reading *Andromeda* on shipboard and admires Euripides' saucy antitheses ("life is not life," and so on), his passionate women, the light melodies of his choruses. To descend into the underworld he borrows a lion skin and a club from the heroic Heracles and continues with his slave Xanthias across the Styx on Charon's ferry. In the underworld river is a chorus of Frogs (beast fable, subhuman) and a chorus of processioners in the Eleusinian mysteries (spiritual, superhuman).[1] They chant the joys of the harvest, the beautiful light of the sun, the probability of sex and fertility.

The journey itself parodies the underworld trip of Odysseus, Heracles, Theseus, and others. There is an inn hostess who remembers Heracles from his lion skin, which Dionysus is wearing, and she welcomes him back. Even in the wonderful realm of the dead one may find the probable forms of life on earth—way stations, dancing girls, egotism, social position (Dionysus argues with Aeacus about aristocracy), money affairs (Charon's two-obol fee is compared to the admission price for the theater). Both the choruses, frogs and mystics, call for Dionysus in his

---

[1] Compare subhuman Caliban, superhuman Ariel in the similar wonderful voyage of *The Tempest*.

other functions as god of mysteries and wine; he is known and hailed before he arrives.

In the contest between Aeschylus and Euripides, the literary devices of parody, accusation, argument, irony, and contrast enrich the criticism of Aristophanes in a way that explicit prose discourse could hardly equal. Topics in literary criticism are superlatively explored by the use of symbols, as the comedies of Molière and certain Restoration plays. In this most effective medium, meanings can be doubled on top of one another in a single statement. For example, Aeschylus' verses weigh more in the mock epic scales than Euripides'—jokingly, because he loads them down with rivers, chariots, and corpses, as opposed to the ships, maces, and dice of Euripides; seriously, Aeschylus' have a greater profundity of both sound and sense, because they are traditional and infinitely symbolic, whereas those of Euripides are finitely conceptual and written according to literary canons originating with himself. Euripides fails to understand Aeschylus' rich symbolic use of connotation and accuses him of verboseness and bombast. Aeschylus, however, is able to tag Euripidean prologues successfully with the comic phrase "lost his little bottle of oil," first, because Euripides' rhythms, original with himself, have monotonous, thin structure of caesura recurrences underneath the actual diversity of metrical forms used; and second, because his logical style does not have an organic unity over an entire speech, and can therefore be interrupted by nonsense without violent shock.

Euripides violates the norms of tradition in both ethics and poetry. He is a rationalist searcher for the wonderful, a nonprobable, fanciful romantic like Shelley. He sees life ultimately as a violent chaos of wars and irrepressible instincts. Like the halcyon, he would escape into the always nonprobable vistas of seas and islands. He is Rousseau as he was at the beginning of the industrial revolution, the unkempt and bitter intellectual romantic, aloof from society yet worshiped by hordes of devotees. His asocial, amoral skepticism and his narrow individuality contrast with the glowing social norms of the old aristocratic–symbolic life. According to Aeschylus and Aristophanes, his thieves, lame beggars, and ragged kings (nonprobable juxtaposition of aristocracy and pariahism) are aesthetically and morally indecorous. They imply unhealthy individualism. Only by the hair-splitting use of logic—Aristophanes, like all comic poets, parodies all logic—can they rationalize their complete abandonment to instinct. Not they, but the lofty symbols of great heroes, are to Aeschylus the proper subjects of tragedy.

Euripides sees art as conceptual liberalism and hedonism (to comic Aristophanes one would imply the other); Aeschylus, as symbolic traditionalism and religious vision. Euripides would reveal the abnormality of actuality in his art as a destructive shock to the mask of convention; Aeschylus would represent the ideal norm as a guide to youth. Aristophanes, who wished, futilely and unwisely—in contrast to the clear-seeing Sophocles—to preserve as it was the harmonious symbolic culture of the old Athens, saw danger in the novelty of concepts which questioned on a logical basis the old values. The essentially materialistic relativism of Euripides and the Sophists could easily destroy these values and cause the settled norms of the traditional life to erupt. The split was coming in the enriching ambiguity of *to kalon,* which meant at once the aesthetically beautiful and the ethically good. Discussion would substitute for vision, fancy for imagination, laws for an ethical code of the tribe. To Aristophanes, degeneration had already set in with the modernism of Euripides and his ilk. The Athenian citizen, symbolized by Dionysus, should return from his hedonistic taste in Euripides to the prophetic vision of Aeschylus.

As the contest progresses, Euripides fails to bait the religious Aeschylus (as he could bait the bourgeois) into saying that Phaedra could not be driven to sin by her unholy love for her stepson Hippolytus. Aeschylus maintains that such sins, however true, should be concealed in the individual conscience, not made the subject of art. Euripides accuses Aeschylus of writing about mountains, rivers, and unreal heroes instead of the men he himself professes to present humanistically; but Aeschylus answers that his own ideal traditionalism is the true education for social man.

Dionysus, who has originally come to the lower world specifically to bring Euripides back to earth, is conscripted as the judge of the dramatic contest and gradually brought to realize the moral superiority of Aeschylus over the dramatist who had hitherto been his favorite. The ultimate test is moral substance in their dramas. Dionysus speaks:

> Now then, whichever of you two shall best
> Advise the city, he shall come with me.
> And first of Alcibiades, let each
> Say what he thinks; the city travails sore.

To this Euripides, after asking Dionysus what the city herself thinks (that is, fishing for a clue), replies:

> I loathe a townsman who is slow to aid
> And swift to hurt, his town; who ways and means
> Finds for himself, but finds not for the state.

But Aeschylus answers immediately:

> 'Twere best to rear no lion in the state,
> But having reared, 'tis best to humour him.

Alcibiades, a degenerate, unscrupulous aristocrat who had twice betrayed the state and indulged violently in drink and homosexuality, was nevertheless a brilliant general, and Athens needed generals. Whether to use his services or to expel him, and how to manage him in either case, was a most perplexing problem for the desperate city in the last years of the war. Euripides, after implicitly asking Dionysus to solve his problem for him, gives in answer a statement which is not only obvious—what moralist, other things being equal, does not hate one who puts his own advantage ahead of society?—but also beside the point. He has stated only one side of the citizen's dilemma, giving no answer to the problem of what specifically to do with Alcibiades. His statement is neatly logical and arranges itself into pretty dichotomies, but is quite useless.

Whereas Euripides' answer is doctrinaire, hence related implicitly only to his own logical system, Aeschylus' is gnomic, hence related implicitly to the traditional wisdom of the racial past. The former governs his conduct by a rationalistic system, the latter by the gradual arrangement of experience into social norms. In contrast to the shallow logic of Euripides'

58

statement, the utterance of Aeschylus is a supralogical perception. He grasps intuitively the problem of Alcibiades in the intense, many-faceted symbol of the lion, which at once expresses the essence of Alcibiades and advises the course of action for the state. The judge must choose Aeschylus.

The plebeian Dionysus, however, makes his judgment not on the probable earth but in the wonderful realm of the underworld, peopled with gods and shades, into which he voyages. It is possible that Aristophanes, who vigorously lampooned the incapacities of the mob mind in the *Wasps, Knights, Clouds,* and *Acharnians,* did not conceive it probable that the normal man in Athenian democracy was capable of such a judgment.

Comedy in the normal joy of its own golden mean expels the abnormality of the dark voyagers. To Aristophanes, Aeschylus is serious insofar as he maintains the social norms of aristocratic life, religion, and the traditional style. In his excess of heroic individuality and pain, he becomes to comedy, like all artists, an object of laughter. So the strictures of Euripides remain about Aeschylus' "ox-hide style," his mouthing verbiage, his diction, which is as excessively luxurious as a Persian tapestry. Aristophanes, significantly, represents Prometheus only as a wretch chained to a rock and gnawed at by vultures.

As the *Frogs* debates old symbol and new concept in poetry through the contest between Aeschylus and Euripides, the *Clouds* does so in philosophy through the debate betwen Just and Unjust Reason. The *Clouds* was produced in 423 after a two-year series of Athenian victories, when Aristophanes could diverge, as in the *Frogs,* from subjects immediately related to the war. In this play Strepsiades (Twister), an old farmer who is fond of Aeschylus, the fruits of rural life, simple family ways, and the old mores, has left the country and married an aristocratic city wife who French-kisses, wears exotic clothes, and loves society life. They represent the two classes of the old tribal life, plebeian and aristocrat, in the new empire. The plebeian husband is unassimilated by the city; he has troubles with money-lenders, law courts, the abstractions of life in an imperialistic metropolis. On the other hand, his aristocratic wife and son are corrupted by the city's pleasures. They overindulge in hedonism where their ances-

59

tors followed the golden mean; the aristocrats of the old tribe were glorious, their descendents in the new city are perverse.

Strepsiades' son, Pheidippides (the name is a comprise between rural "thrift" and aristocratic "horse") has gone to excess in spending money on horses. In the opening scene he talks race-track jargon in his sleep as his rustic father worries about his debts for expensive horses. Seeking to avoid paying at least the interest, Strepsiades hits on the plan of learning tricks of logic from the sophistic science-researcher Socrates. Led by a pale and ragged devotee, he is admitted into the Thinkery of Socrates, which is compared to the wonderful realm of the dead. The master is indulging in useless speculation, treading air and contemplating the sun. Strepsiades has interrupted his research into the footprints of fleas and the bowels of gnats. Though Socrates tries to teach him, the old farmer forgets easily. His limited mind can think only in concrete, empirical terms. He can see "measures" only as pints and gallons, not as part of poetic theory, and wants to destroy the abstract certificates of debt with a scientific burning glass. But he rapidly picks up the surface clichés of the new concepts. He denounces the gods to everybody, after Socrates, by the characteristically comic use of perverted logic, proves to him that the clouds, not Zeus, cause rain, and that the Whirl of Anaxagoras' and Empedocles' scientific theories, not the symbols of the old gods, rules in the universe.

Socrates finally gives up in disgust with the old man; Strepsiades must persuade Pheidippides to learn the new tricks of argument, or he will have to pay his son's debts. The son learns too well and overthrows the probable, tribal wisdom of manners toward the older generation for the neat logic of social concepts. His father whipped Pheidippides in childhood; what more logical than that he should whip his father in second childhood? Strepsiades himself manages to jumble all the ideas of Socrates and get rid of his creditors, but Pheidippides' extreme use of the Unjust Reason to make the worse appear the better cause persuades the old man to resume his faith in Zeus. He runs wild upon the Thinkery of Socrates, burns it down, and administers beatings to the disciples. With joy of success in this undertaking, the play closes.

The complexities and concepts of the new Empire completely bewilder the rustic Strepsiades; even when he tries to utilize them to his own ends, they backfire. They are antagonistic towards him, the symbolic destroyers of his way of life. He sees the speculation of science as useless knowledge, and being selfish, like all comic characters, after he can no longer benefit from it he rejects the Machiavellian use of logic in business affairs. Only his son is able to master this, but he can do it precisely because he is a corrupt hedonist, like Euripides whom he admires. To Aristophanes, though everybody is basically selfish, only amorality will be able to twist concepts selfishly to its own ends. Further, all conceptual thinkers, motivated selfishly when seen in social, probable terms, cannot be other than immoral. When logic is allowed full sway, it can easily defeat the instinctively correct norms of social thought which have accumulated over the history of the tribe. The Unjust (worse) Reason, by the use of its conceptual logic argues that it will educate Pheidippides to amoralism:

> (To the Just, better Reason) Get you gone, you are but an old fool. (To Pheidippides) But you, young man, just consider a little what this temperance means, and the delights of which it deprives you— young fellows, women, play, dainty dishes, wine, boisterous laughter. And what is life worth without these? Then, if you happen to commit one of these faults inherent in human weakness, some seduction or adultery, and you are caught in the act, you are lost, if you cannot speak [that is, like the sophists]. But follow my teaching and you will be able to satisfy your passions, to dance, to laugh, to blush at nothing. Suppose you are caught in the act of adultery. Then up and tell the husband you are not guilty, and recall to him the example of Zeus, who allowed himself to be conquered by love and by women. Being but a mortal, can you be stronger than a god?

By such "Socratic" logic and Euripidean relativism the Unjust Reason easily controverts the Just Reason, which vainly praises the norms of the old religious life:

> Very well, I will tell you what was the old education, when I used to teach justice with so much success and when modesty was held in veneration. First, it was required of a child that it should not utter a word. In the street, when they went to the music school, all the youths

of the same district marched lightly clad and ranged in good order, even when the snow was falling in great flakes. . . . They were taught to sing either "Pallas, the Terrible, who overturneth cities," or "A noise resounded from afar," in the solemn tones of the ancient harmony. If anyone indulged in buffoonery or lent his voice any of the soft inflexions, like those which today the disciples of Phrynis take so much pains to form, he was treated as an enemy of the Muses and belaboured with blows. . . . They were not to be seen approaching a lover and themselves rousing his passion by soft modulation of the voice and lustful gaze. At table, they would not have dared, before those older than themselves, to have taken a radish, an aniseed or a leaf of parsley, and much less eat fish or thrushes, or cross their legs.

Comedy is probable, normal, and conservative. It expels the abnormal intellectual. Socrates to the conservative comedian is a threat to the norms who will bring chaos out of order with all sorts of new and impractical schemes; he must therefore be defeated. This was the social opinion also of the Athenian people, who put Socrates to death twenty-four years after their symbol Strepsiades had set fire to his laboratory—and on the same charge: "corrupting the youth."

Socrates in the *Clouds* is credited with only two modes of thought (neither of which, if we are to believe Plato, he practised): fruitless scientific investigation, and Machiavellian sophism; one useless, the other diabolical. In the renaissance of the sixth century B.C. a number of cosmological theories developed and scientific research was undertaken for its own sake on inductive principles. The popular Greek mind associated this conceptual thought with a denial of the traditional gods,—correctly in the case of Xenophanes and Protagoras. The popular mind further associated all original thought in the form of concepts with science, and judged it impious. This was a charge they later made against Socrates, whose ideas were more religious than scientific; and in the *Clouds* he is falsely represented as a follower of the theories of Thales, Empedocles, and Anaxagoras, a contriver of impractical experiments and contemplator of empty ideas who worships Whirl and the clouds instead of Zeus and the gods.

The extension of trade and the development of international politics gave rise also to new rationales of diplomatic action. The Machiavellian type of politician emerged, as it does in any expanding empire. Like our own social psychologists, the sophists delineated the probable norms of governing men in masses. They sold their techniques to ambitious young statesmen who desired to mold public opinion by rhetoric. In the pure action of such government, logic, merely a probable tool for selfish ends, becomes diabolical, and philosophy becomes a joke. Aristophanes represents Socrates as a corrupter of the youth, a sophist who teaches logic as part of the technique of handling probabilities in human situations. He is, to Aristophanes, the official philosopher of the amoralism and corruption in the new empire.

In the limited, provincial governments of the old tribes, there were two classes, aristocrats and farmers. The aristocrats set the patterns of morals, and the farmers followed. But in the new commerce of international empire, the aristocracy became effete and amoral through excessive leisure and luxury, like Strepsiades' wife and his son Pheidippides. Those who held the power of commerce and government were the unscrupulous pupils of the sophists; whether their origins were humble, like Cleon's, or aristocratic, like Alcibiades', they were not interested in guiding the state. They merely manipulated the democratic mob to their own ends. The one hope of the new empire was the altruistic intellectual, who was also a product of the renaissance. The self-conscious objectivity of this new conceptualism, whether it deepened the old religion, as with Sophocles, or followed paths of free thought, as with Socrates, could have substituted for the pure action of the old aristocracy as a rational norm and guide for the people. The tragedy is that the people, as was probable by their old social norms, responded by rejecting the abnormal intellectuals who alone could have saved their empire from ruin. Even when the empirical rustic minds of these people wanted, like Strepsiades, to use logic for selfish ends, they were unable to understand, and they mistrusted anyone who could, except those who were clever enough to flatter them. While the non-probable intellectual was concerned with the wonderful ideas of individual ethics, the Machiavellian politicians were decisively manipulating the mob by their probable techniques. Athens loved Cleon and Alcibiades, but executed Socrates; the *Clouds* of Aristophanes both misunderstands and rejects him. This play is the supreme indictment of the comic view of life, the normal, social, and probable from which all that diverges will be expelled, even the near saint.

Critics who are driven by the wish to make life come out all right will always ignore the deep contradiction between society and individual implied by the *Clouds* and seek to channel the implications of Aristophanes into more shallow currents. He meant it all in fun, they will argue, and point to the delicate humor of Plato's *Symposium*. But the implications are unambiguous of a social comedy which misrepresents and misunderstands an individual thinker, shows him as a selfish pariah both unscrupulous and excessively theoretical, and finally burns his laboratory in an orgy of self-satisfaction. If there is any doubt of this, Socrates himself says in the *Apology* that the *Clouds* spread the very ideas about him which led to his execution:

> But far more dangerous [than his present accusers] are these, who began when you were children [*Clouds,* 423 B.C., trial, 399], and took possession of your minds with their falsehoods, telling of one Socrates, a wise man, who speculated about the heaven above, and searched into the earth beneath, and made the worse appear the better cause [the precise charges of the *Clouds*]. These are the accusers whom I dread; for they are the circulators of this rumor, and their hearers are too apt to fancy that speculators of this sort do not believe in the gods. And they are many, and their charges against me are of ancient date, and they made them in days when you were impressible, . . . and the cause when heard went by default, for there was none to answer. And hardest of all, their names I do not know and cannot tell; unless in the chance case of a comic poet.

Those who wish to interpret the tragic irony of the last sentence as a merry chuckle are welcome to do so.

PEACE, WAR, AND EMPIRE · *ACHARNIANS* AND *PEACE*

Aristophanes' first extant play, the *Acharnians* (425 B.C.), works out attitudes toward the Peloponnesian War among various members of the older generation—the chorus of rustic charcoal burners from the country district of Acharnae; Dikaiopolis (just-city), the protagonist, who lives in the country but has assimilated the ways of the urban empire; and Lamachus, a warrior of aristocratic origin who has degenerated into the blood-lusting professional soldier, a comic General Patton.

Dikaiopolis at the beginning of the play has come early to the Assembly. He awaits the crowd of citizens who will linger in the market place till the sergeant-at-arms comes through with a freshly painted rope and then jostle one another to get the best seats. The old man, heartsick with war, yearns for the blessings of peace.

An aristocratic Persian envoy, King's Eye, enters, who turns out to be the homosexual Cleisthenes (symbolizing how the excess of Asian luxury in the days of Aeschylus produced the decadent fifth-century aristocracy). Dikaiopolis feels sorry for the plebeian naval rowers, the saviors of the city, who would be indignant at the high pay and luxurious living of these aristocratic Persian ambassadors.

On the sly, he bargains with Theorus, the Spartan ambassador, for a bottle of the precious peace liquid. Both are pursued by the outraged Acharnian charcoal burners, veterans of Marathon who feel a blind patriotism in any war, whether the defense against Persia or the imperialistic rivalry of Athens with Sparta. Dikaiopolis, however, makes a convincing speech to them and persuades them he is right after winning an argument with the chauvinistic Lamachus. The old farmer wins everywhere. He buys from a starving Megarian (neighboring Athens held a strict blockade on Megara) his two daughters disguised as sacrificial pigs. He gets a lush Copaic eel from a wealthy Boeotian, plans a feast of meat and fruits, gives a drop of the precious peace liquid to a bride for her groom's phallus. The wild procession at the end of the play contrasts the wounded Lamachus in his armor with the feasting Dikaiopolis with a slave girl on either arm; the sterility, pain, and metal arms of war with the grapes, meats, and fruitful sex of peace.

Dikaiopolis is the very type of eternally successful comic hero. More specifically, he symbolizes the possibility for the plebeian masses, rustic in origin, of becoming the politically aware citizens of the new Athenian democracy. The old charcoal burners, too feeble now for war, see things only from the rustic, tribal point of view. They are absorbed in the tasks of the farm; war to them means trampled grapes, broken vine poles, and perhaps a son gloriously fighting overseas for a state which seems to them the same that it was at the time of Marathon. The abstractions of the new impersonal machinery of government and law they do not understand. In the law courts a rhetorical young sophist "with twisted words" has fleeced some helpless old fellow of the money he had hoarded for his coffin.

But Dikaiopolis, keeping his ties with the old symbolic culture, can still acquire the techniques of the new conceptual machinery. He is a family man rooted in country ways, a healthy old husband who still enjoys the natural pleasures of food and sex. His favorite poet is Aeschylus, yet he goes to the house of Euripides and wheedles some rags, greens, and candles from that shabby recluse to use for his trial. He keeps his own garden, yet attends the law courts. His interests are patriotic, yet he sees how inevitable and futile it is for two empires to be hostile towards one another. Everybody wants peace, but he alone is able to operate and achieve it.

His success is contrasted with the failures of the Acharnians, chained to their plebeian rusticity, and of Lamachus, blind in his professional soldiery. While the Acharnians cower before the aristocratic Lamachus, Dikaiopolis asks him for a feather to help him vomit into the aristocrat's helmet; when Lamachus calls him a beggar (which he would have been in the old tribal state), he answers that he is a citizen. He is not awed by the luxurious trappings of Lamachus' armor. The degeneration of aristocracy, implicit in the fact that their sphere has narrowed to soldiery as a profession, is clearly shown in the clandestine hedonism of Lamachus, who tries to buy secretly through the agency of his servant a Copaic eel from Dikaiopolis.

The *Peace,* produced in 421, just before the truce between Athens and Sparta, reflects the same ideas as the *Acharnians.* Trygaios is an old farmer like Dikaiopolis, and the chorus of farmers, like the Acharnians, are rustic tillers of the soil. When they say that the moment is unpropitious for peace, Trygaios replies that peace must come at some time and the fully ripe moment never comes. His slaves at the beginning of the play are nourishing a cantankerous dung beetle, huge as a pack ass, which Trygaios rides to heaven to bring back the maiden Peace for his fellow citizens. As Dikaiopolis argues with Lamachus, so Trygaios argues with Hermes, the messenger of the gods, whom he meets in heaven. The god War desires to keep hostility alive; he mixes it continually like a salad. But Spartan Brasidas and Athenian Cleon, the mortar and pestle of his war saladbowl, have both died the year before at the battle of Amphipolis. Trygaios is finally successful in winning Peace, and along with her the maidens Mayfair and Harvesthome. Freed of packsacks, rations, and ornately armoured generals, Athens will again be fruitful with love-making, grapes, eels, cheesecakes, roast oxen, all the plenty of peace:

> Cause the Greeks once more to taste the pleasant beverage of friend-ship and temper all hearts with the gentle feeling of forgiveness. Make excellent commodities flow to our markets, fine heads of garlic, early cucumbers, apples, pomegranates, and nice little cloaks for the slaves; make them bring geese, ducks, pigeons, and larks from Boeotia and baskets of eels from Lake Copais; we shall all rush to buy them, dis-puting their possession with Morychus, Teleas, Glaucetes, and every other glutton.

While Trygaios is preparing a sacrifice of meats for Peace, he is beset by a conservative priest. True to his origins in the old culture, he quotes both parodied and actual lines from Homer against the Brahmin-like traditionalism of the priest's arguments, and finally drives him away without any food. He rejoices in the new prosperity of the Sickle-maker, breaks spears for vine poles and uses armor for toilet bowls. The sons of Lamachus the braggart soldier and Cleonymos the coward (both sym-bolically following in their fathers' footsteps) are dismissed at once. After dispersing the disappointed war profiteers, sellers of helmets, breastplates, crests, and oracles, he and the chorus dance in an orgy of sex and feasting.

In these plays Aristophanes discusses political alternatives solely in terms of the older generation's ideals; Dikaiopolis and Trygaios, both old farmers, understand the wars of the new empire and successfully utilize all means to achieve the bounteousness of peace for their city. In the other political plays written before the *Birds*—the *Knights* (424) and the *Wasps* (422)—he shows in concrete political terms the tension between the tribal religion of the older generation and the new conceptual thought of the youth.

POLITICS AND THE MACHINERY OF GOVERNMENT · *KNIGHTS* AND *WASPS*

After the death of Pericles (429 B.C.) there were two main parties in Athens, the agriculturalist peace party led by Nicias and the city. war party led by Cleon. Nicias, superstitious, timid, and old-fashioned, was no match for the demagogue Cleon, who had mastered the sophistic techniques of maneuvering public opinion. The *Knights,* produced shortly after the battle of Sphacteria (425), attacks Cleon at the height of his favor and rule.

In the *Knights,* the old man Demos (the People) has two slaves, Nicias and Demosthenes (the general of Sphacteria). They complain about the wiles of a third newly bought slave, the Splutterer (Cleon), with their master. Searching for someone of even lower plebeian origins and cleverer pure-action strategy than Cleon, they steal an oracle which the Splutterer has and find that he will be ousted by a Sausage-Seller. Just then they run across a hard-bitten vendor of sausages who has spent his boyhood bustling around the markets of the harbor. He has so little of the old education that he is at a complete loss to understand the symbolic oracle:

DEMOSTHENES.
> *You shall become, this oracle declares,*
> *A man most mighty.*

SAUSAGE-SELLER.   *Tell me, then, how I,*
> *A sausage-seller, can become a man.*

DEM. *Why, that's the very thing will make you great,*
> *Your roguery, impudence, and market-training.*

S.-S. *I am not worthy of great power, I think.*

DEM. *What's that? Not worthy? What's the matter now?*
You've got, I fear, some good upon your conscience.
Spring you from gentlemen?
S.-S. *By the gods, not I;*
From utter wretches.
DEM. *Lucky, lucky man,*
O what a start you've got for public life!
S.-S. *But, friend, I know no culture, just the letters.*
And even of them but little, and that badly.
DEM. *. . . To be a people-leader is not now*
For cultured men, nor yet for honest men,
But for the base and ignorant.

And the Sausage-Seller elsewhere describes his plebeian education:

Now by the knuckles which in youth would discipline my head,
And those hard-handled butchers' knives they often used instead,
. . . And lots of other obscene tricks I practiced as a boy.
O how I used to chouse the cooks by shrieking out AHOY!
Look lads, a swallow! spring is here, look up, look up, I pray;
So up they looked whilst I purloined a piece of meat away,
And no one caught me out, or else, if any saw me pot it
I clapped the meat between my thighs and vowed I hadn't got it.
Whereat an orator observed who watched me at my tricks,
"Some day this boy will make his mark as leader on the Pnyx."

The trainer of demagogues realizes that this scrabbler in the urban market place will be unscrupulous enough to sway the Assembly.

The debate between Cleon and the Sausage-Seller must culminate in a decision by the master Demos (the people) as to which pleases him more. Cleon in the rush of argument admits that he considers the citizenry a social mass to be molded, not a group of thinking individuals. He plays for probable power and is not interested in individual problems: "O people . . . nought did I care how a townsman might fare as long as I satisfied you." During the debate, Demos wavers between one and the other, though he slowly inclines toward the Sausage-Seller, who promises him the concrete joy of meats and fruits in answer to the abstract wealth promised by Cleon. It turns out that the Sausage-Seller's signet is a fig leaf stuffed with the fat of roast ox, whereas that of Cleon is a cormorant haranguing the crowd from a rock. The selfish fickleness of the crowd and Cleon's shameless pandering to it are revealed in a rain of jokes and symbols. The two vie to give Demos meat, soup, honey cake, fish, and porridge. Finally, the contest is decided when, after both Sausage-Seller and Cleon have proferred gifts in succession for some time, the packs of both are examined:

> S.-S. *I'll tell you what; steal softly up, and search*
> *My hamper first, then Splutterer's, and note*
> *What's in them; then you'll surely judge aright.*
>
> DEM. *Well, what does* yours *contain?*
>
> S.-S. *See here, it's empty,*
> *Dear Father mine, I served up all for you.*
>
> DEM. *A Demos-loving hamper, sure enough.*
>
> S.-S. *Now come along, and look at Splutterer's.*
> *Hey, only see. . . .*
>
> DEM. *Why, here's a store of dainties!*
> *Why, here's a splendid cheesecake he put by!*
> *And me he gave the tiniest slice, so big.*
>
> S.-S. *And, Demos, that is what he always does;*
> *Gives you the pettiest morsel of his gains*
> *And keeps by far the largest share himself.*

Cleon, of course, has actually accumulated an imposing fortune in the public service. The Sausage-Seller instructs Demos in his past errors, his selfishness, his gullibility to demagogues like Cleon and Hyperbolus; he is retained as the chief servant of Demos, while Cleon is packed off at the end of the play to the Sausage-Seller's old job in the market place, with the ignominious added duty of cleaning up after prostitutes. Comedy represents the success of society over the clever individual; if the slick Cleon is temporarily able to sway society, it will always produce a humble Sausage-Seller to overcome him.

The *Knights,* second in chronological order of the extant plays, is at once the most optimistic and the least satisfying of Aristophanes' political plays. The success does not really work itself out through the symbolic resolution of problems. It is a mere formula. The pariah Sausage-Seller, the unscrupulous Cleon, Demosthenes, the wavering Nicias, the aristocratic Knights, Demos the people—all become happy, normal, and harmonious on the surface, without having to work out symbolically in probable terms the tensions which exist among them as diverse members of a single changing society. The Sausage-Seller is no improvement on Cleon, despite his not-too-convincing altruism at the end of the play; he is able to defeat Cleon only because he is more unscrupulous.

The vote of the citizen body at large was the greatest single problem of the Athenian democracy. And it is the one which Aristophanes treats least realistically; perhaps because comedy must shut its eyes to the paradox of its own society's tragic implications; or rather, it must ritually destroy the paradox by denying its existence. Aristophanes is more satisfying in the *Wasps* (422), where he explores the reaction of the young generation and the old to the more specific problem of legal machinery.

With the rise of commerce, colonization, and international empire in Athens came a highly developed impersonal machinery of justice. The entire democratic citizen body over the age of thirty was eligible for jury service, and the annual enrollment was set at six thousand. This gave the people at large a potent weapon, which is symbolized by the stings in the "tails" of the Wasps, the old jurors who comprise the chorus of this play.

The battle between the old generation and the new is clearly represented in the *Wasps,* as in the *Clouds,* by the opposition of father and son in one family. The young son Bdelycleon (Loathe-Cleon) successfully masters both the old culture and the new. He feasts his father, dresses him in aristocratic garments, and shows himself well acquainted with the ethics and literature of the symbolic past; yet he has been raised in the city and possesses an awareness of the concepts and government of the new empire. His father Philocleon (Love-Cleon), a rustic whose habits have not been formed in the city, is unbalanced by the flattering non-probable novelty of having governmental power. Cleon is able to mold the old Philocleon and his generation, because their instinctual thought can be probably anticipated. Proud of their rustic virtue and their service in the old Persian War, they remain as old men completely hedonistic. Their power in the law court flatters their ego, and the juror's fee which Cleon raised to over half the wage of a normal working man attracts them even more; they spend all their time in the court.

The wise young Bdelycleon decides to curb the excess of his law-infatuated father by restraining old Philocleon in the house. Two slaves bidden to keep watch at the front door discuss the old man at dawn as the play opens. One comments on his dream of the overwhelming crowd of jurors and their plasticity in the hands of Cleon:

> *'Twas in my earliest sleep I thought I saw*
> *A flock of sheep assembled on Pnyx hill,*
> *Sitting close-packed, with little cloaks and staves;*
> *Then to these sheep I heard, or seemed to hear*
> *An all-receptive grampus holding forth*
> *In tone and accents like a scalded pig.*

Old Philocleon, stubbing his toe, tries to steal out of the house by clinging beneath a pack ass, as Odysseus had escaped from Polyphemus' cave by clinging under a ram. But young Bdelycleon knows his Homer too well, and the ruse fails. At last the chorus of Wasps, with the sting of their collective social power, comes to the house to carry the old man off. They identify the moral Bdelycleon with the amoral Alcibiades, because both are masters of the new ideas, and accuse the young man of conspiring for tyranny. They cannot understand that the young "radical" is less foolish about government than they are. His superficial abnormalities—long hair and the wrong fashions in clothes—shock them:

> BDELYCLEON.
> *Can't we now, without this outcry*
> *and this fierce denunciation*
> *Come to peaceful terms together—*
> *terms of reconciliation?*

72

Wasps.
> Terms with you, you people-hater,
>   and with Brasidas, you traitor,
> Hand and glove. You who dare
>   Wooly-fringed clothes to wear,
> Yes, and show beard and hair
>   left to grow everywhere.

In the ensuing argument, Bdelycleon offers his old father luxurious clothes and feasts if he will give up the jury trials. The son wants to make an aristocrat out of the old man, to endow him with manners and culture. But his father, not content with these merely sensual pleasures, craves also the ego-satisfaction of power of judgment in the court. Philocleon asks if he commits an individual sin in judging; Bdelycleon answers that his type is, rather, a social disgrace. The young man grows weary of the struggle to break the rustic habits of a lifetime:

> Hard were the task, and shrewd the intent,
>   —for a comedy-poet all too great—
> To attempt to heal an inveterate, old
>   disease engrained in the heart of the state.

At last Bdelycleon persuades his father to stay home in a private make-shift court to judge the case of the dog Snatch, who has stolen a large fish from the kitchen. The mock trial is carried through in all formality. At the end Bdelycleon plays grossly on Philocleon's sympathy and leads him by swiftly shifting the voting urns to acquit the dog. The old man through this action is made to realize the social implications of his individual vacillations. As in the *Knights,* the point is implied that social norms are only the generalized total of many individuals, each of whom must be responsible for his own actions. Philocleon totters under the new awareness that hitherto he has dodged this responsibility. After he has been tricked into placing his ballot of decision in the wrong box, he asks (though he is the only voter!),

Well, how went the battle?

BDEL.	*We shall soon see. O Snatch, you are acquitted!*
	Why, how now, father?
PHIL.	*Water, give me water!*
BDEL.	*Hold up sir, do.*
PHIL.	*Just tell me this,*
	Is he indeed acquitted?
BDEL.	*Yes.*
PHIL.	*I'm done for.*
BDEL.	*Don't take it so to heart; stand up, sir, pray.*
PHIL.	*How shall I bear this sin upon my soul?*
	A man acquitted! What awaits me now?
	Yet, O great gods, I pray you pardon me;
	Unwilling I did it, not from natural bent.

The chorus continues to boast of its service in the Persian Wars, assuming it a natural right that they should enjoy the jury courts in their old age; but Bdelycleon succeeds in clothing his father in aristocratic garments and winning him from his old passion. Still, he cannot teach Philocleon the old symbolic myths; the old man enjoys the songs of Phrynicus but his chief delights are the plebeian animal fables of Aesop and dirty stories. Nay, tell me no legends, he says; give me something human.

Philocleon seems finally to realize how he has been duped by Cleon, and settles for the sensual pleasures of sex and a banquet. After this, a female breadseller fails to involve him in an accusation of assault. All catch a mess of "golden-crested wrens," and dance off for a happy feast.

In this play Aristophanes places his hope in the moral members of the younger generation who are wise enough to realize the basic virtues of the old tribal norms in ethics and culture. The intellectuality of Bdelycleon emerges victorious over the instinctive selfishness of his rustic father, despite the sympathy of the audience for the old man throughout the play.

THE IDEAL STATE · *BIRDS* AND *ECCLESIAZUSAE*

The increasing bitterness of the war and the development of Aristophanes' own genius combined to make his plays more directly symbolic. His imagination had always been fertile in verbal symbols and descriptions; he came gradually to use it in the unraveling of the action itself.

In the *Birds* (414), the self-sufficient Peisthetairos (Persuade-Your-Companion) and his friend Euelpides (Fair-Hope) have left Athens and her crowded law courts to search for the wonderful kingdom of the birds. Its king, Tereus the Hoopoe, has left in his past the tragic events of Sophocles' *Tereus*. The heavy guilt that hung over his house in the tragedy has melted comically into domestic felicity; he lives happily with his old wife Procne, now a nightingale. As the kingdom of the birds is wonderful to the travelers, so they as strangers are wonderful to the Hoopoe and his subjects. They must try one another in the social intercourse of conversation. Are you looking for a better city than Athens?, asks the Hoopoe; then you must want an aristocracy. Least of all that, says Peisthetairos; it turns out that he wants to escape the probabilities of social mores for a riotous individualism, yet a perfectly harmonious state. The Hoopoe suggests several cities, but Peisthetairos desires a completely nonprobable bird kingdom in the air built like Babylon with walls of brick.

After the hostility of the bird chorus has been calmed, Peisthetairos explains that the birds in the mid-region of the air could starve out the gods in heaven by stopping the fumes of sacrifice. The birds would then rule all from the new Cloudcuckooland.

Quoting not the tragic-aristocratic Homer, but the plebeian Aesop, Peisthetairos explains in a parody of logic how the birds were the first gods. In a mockery of traditionalism, he cites the probable Athenian customs about birds, while the birds themselves, parodying the *Theogony* of Hesiod, construct a symbolic myth of the world's origin:

> *There was Chaos at first, and Darkness and Night*
> > *and Tartarus vasty and dismal,*
> *But the Earth was not there, nor the Sky, nor the Air*
> > *till at length in the bosom abysmal*
> *Of Darkness an egg, from the whirlwind conceived*
> > *was laid by the sable-plumed Night.*
> *And out of that egg, as the Seasons revolved, sprang Love,*
> > *the entrancing, the bright,*
> *Love brilliant and bold with his pinions of gold,*
> > *like a whirlwind, refulgent and sparkling.*

Love hatched us; commingling in Tartarus wide,
with Chaos, with murky, the darkling.
And brought us above, as the firstlings of love,
and first to the light we ascended.
There was never a race of immortals at all
till Love had the universe blended.

.   .   .   .

So we than the Blessed are older by far;
and abundance of proof is existing
That we are the children of Love, for we fly
unfortunate lovers assisting.

No sooner have Peisthetairos and the Hoopoe instituted the wonderful Cloudcuckooland than they are besieged by the probable difficulties of all new states—flocks of undesirable aliens. The worst pariahs and slickest opportunists rush immediately to the new city: a priest, a poet, a seller of oracles, a theoretical technician who will measure out the area of the new city, a statue seller, hedonistic aesthetes who love the new poetry. Peisthetairos, the successful comic hero, cleverly anticipates the norms of these characters before they can deceive him, and dispatches them. As they proceed to build Cloudcuckooland, with various birds doing tasks fitted to them, the immortals begin to arrive. Iris, the rainbow messenger of the gods, leaves at once when Peisthetairos threatens to rape her after she tries to argue theology with him. Then the citizens of Athens send a messenger to Peisthetairos with a golden crown for his wisdom.

The birds have become a fad in war-plagued Athens; everybody is given a bird nickname, and children are being named for birds. A beater of his father, thinking that such a practice is honored among the birds, travels joyously to the new city. Peisthetairos, by the sleight of false logic, converts him into a moral citizen. He even finds use for a sycophant whom he tames by his logic.

Prometheus sneaks in, cowering from Zeus beneath an umbrella, and advises what terms to ask of the gods who will shortly come to seek a truce; Zeus should be required to hand over his sceptre and the maiden

Kingship. Then hungry Heracles, Poseidon, and the barbaric god Triballos arrive in a delegation. Peisthetairos nonprobably juxtaposes myth and law by interpreting Heracles' family relations to Zeus in terms of the Athenian legal code, telling him that as a bastard he cannot inherit. This sophistic logic serves to quell the hero and win him from his father Zeus to the cause of the birds. Not least of arguments to the starving gods is the feast which Peisthetairos purposely prepares all during the discussion. At length the clever Athenian gets his terms, and as usual a successful feast of victory ends the play.

This play's myriad parodies—of Homer, Hesiod, Aeschylus, the lyric poets, Sophocles, Euripides, jury systems, philosophy—reflect symbolically all the tensions of the Athenian empire. The relation of old norms to new, abstract speculation and sophistic pure action, plebeianism and aristocracy, the efficient management and business economy of the city, and the personal morals and fertility of the country—all this is symbolically united into success by the comic hero Peisthetairos. He is a comic Faust, an idealistic searcher who ends in the practical norms of politics. Only in the freedom of imaginatively unfolding symbols could the mature Aristophanes reflect so many facets of the central Athenian problem.

The *Ecclesiazusae* (393 B. c.), places the ideal state in Athens itself by having the women take over the reins of government. In this play the contrast between habitual norms of experience and logical abstractions is interwoven with the opposition of the sexes and the ritual dispute between the old and the new.

Praxagora, the intellectual wife of middle-aged Blepyros, has gathered her female companions secretly to the Assembly at dawn. Clad in false beards, and simulating male rhetorical practices, they deliberate handing the state over to women. Inexperience, the conservative characteristics of their sex, and their basic dependence on men show through the futuristic socialist guise of their speeches. Habits are hard to break; one woman wants to do her sewing in the Assembly, they continually swear by the old gods, despite Praxagora's scolding, and she herself, true to the habit of her sex, swear by Demeter and Persephone later in the play. In a parody of logic, she proves that women could govern the state better than men (as well as men—just like men is ambiguously understood throughout). The morality of the past blends with the ideal of the future in contrast to the decadence of the present:

> None would have stooped
> Money to take for
> Attending the meetings, but
> Hither they trooped,
> Each with his own little
> Goatskin of wine,
> Each with three olives, two
> Onions, one loaf, in his
> Wallet, to dine.
> But now they are set
> The three-obol to get,
> And whene'er the State business engages
> They clamor like hodmen for wages.

The rustic symbol of food contrasts with the urban abstraction of money.

Flouting the experiential norms of economic life, Praxagora has a novel scheme for making everybody equally rich:

> The rule which I dare to enact and declare,
> Is that all shall be equal, and equally share
> All wealth and enjoyments, nor longer endure
> That one should be rich and another be poor,
> That one should have acres, far-stretching and wide,
> And another not even enough to provide
> Himself with a grave: that this at his call
> Should have hundreds of servants, and that none at all.
> All this I intend to correct and amend:
> Now all of all blessings shall freely partake,
> One life and one system for all men I make.

The essential problem of distribution of labor she ignores. The slaves will do all the work, she says.

Further, all men and all women will live in a community of free love;

78

and when a young man desires to have intercourse with a young girl, he must first do so with an old or ugly woman.

The play proceeds with the operation of these two schemes. Two citizens, one more liberal than the other, argue as to whether they should really put their goods into common stock. A communal dinner, to be run like a lottery with tickets for food, is announced. Red tape would be even greater in the new state than in the old.

Contrasting with the conceptual social schemes of Praxagora, the ancient ritual norms are represented in the Old–Young debate at the end of the play. An old woman is trying desperately to take a young man from a young girl, and they attack one another in antiphonal debate. Other old women arrive on the scene, who tear the unfortunate youth between them and finally drag him off. As usual, the play ends in a festive procession.

It need hardly be said that this little resembles Plato's *Republic*. The *Ecclesiazusae* presents the comic view of all abstract social systems. In Athens or America, the average man associates only two ideas with any sort of socialism: the equal distribution of goods and free love. Since both violate the norms of social experience and the probably selfish motivation of the majority of men, the normal person concludes that socialism is unpragmatically foolish. This illogical train of thought explains itself only as the comic expulsion of the abnormal intellectual from society; it is the ritual preservation of the norm by deliberate misunderstanding.

Throughout the play the radicals are continually bumping against the norms of habit and violating the basic principle of economics, the law of least possible effort for a given result. Aristophanes at the end of his career (this is his last play but one) and after the defeat of Athens concerned himself only incidentally with the symbolic tensions of the warring democracy. He slipped into an easy satire about general human norms.

WOMEN IN THE NEW EMPIRE · *LYSISTRATA* AND *THESMOPHORIAZUSAE*

As the progress of the war became more hopeless, Aristophanes became more escapist. In the two plays following the *Birds,* after the tremendous disaster of the Sicilian campaign had shaken the city, he placed the tension between old and new in a basic sexual struggle, which is closer to ritual origins but less profound for drama than his earlier explorations of the old–new tension. The *Lysistrata* (411) and the *Thesmophoriazusae* (410) treat respectively the war–peace problem of the *Acharnians* and the religion–conceptualism of the *Frogs* in terms of the man–woman split.

In the play to which she gives the title, Lysistrata (Disbander of Armies) meets at dawn with her women on the Acropolis and unfolds a plan whereby they may stop the ruinous war between Athens and Sparta. The battles of Ares are always opposed to the peaceful rites of Aphrodite; when husbands and sons are slain in battle, when wives have slept alone for years and maidens grow old without the prospect of marriage, something must be done. The almost masculine Lysistrata (there seems to be a touch of Lesbianism in her, as in her fondling of the other women) gathers members of her sex from all warring cities, including Sparta, and declares that the only way to stop war is to refuse their husbands intercourse.

Lysistrata successfully foils an envoy who tries to outargue her. The men become desperate under the proclamation, and finally decide to make peace. While the men offer money (abstraction of new commerce), and the women offer food (concreteness of old fertility), they dance off to a feast and a marriage. Here the conceptual plan in the hands of the women has conquered the most probable norm of all, intercourse between the sexes. The *Lysistrata* is full of jokes against the nonprobability of countering the sex instinct, and the proclamation itself is violated by more than one woman. Yet peace is achieved, Sparta and Athens are united, everybody is made happy. The lusty savor of this play and its escapist failure to solve problems both spring from the deprivations and disappointments of a war which in seven years was to culminate in permanent defeat.

The *Thesmophoriazusae* is presented as taking place during the ancient spring fertility rite of the Thesmophoria (bearers of offerings) to Demeter and Persephone, goddesses of the harvest and the spring rebirth of life. In the secret rites of their festival, the women decide to punish Euripides who has unveiled/maligned their sex. (An ambiguity, reflecting that of bourgeois mask/instinctive reality, is implied throughout.) Euripides, learning of this, first approaches the modernistic tragic poet Agathon, a homosexual aesthete, and asks him to disguise himself as a woman in the rites and argue on Euripides' behalf. Failing to persuade Agathon, he lights on his brother-in-law Mnesilochus, dresses him in women's garments, and packs him off to the Thesmophoria. Aeschylus in the *Frogs* freely admits that Phaedra's passion for her stepson is a probable fact, but the bourgeois women in the *Thesmophoriazusae* are easily led into self-contradiction and defeat by denying this. Angry at Mnesilochus for his arguments, they discover that he is a man and will inflict punishment on him, but he snatches a baby as hostage and stands apart. The baby which a normal old-fashioned woman would carry turns out to be a disguise for the wine bottle of the modern degenerate woman. When Mnesilochus drains the flask, they beset him. In an attempt to be rescued, he adopts a ruse from the *Palamedes* of Euripides by writing a message on the ritual tablets. Unaided, he tries another scheme from the *Helen*. Finally, strapped to a board and about to be punished by a giant Scythian policeman, he sings a parody lament to night, like that of Euripides' Andromeda on the rock. Euripides himself enters like the rescuing Perseus, seduces the policeman with a dancing girl, and makes off successfully with his kinsman by offering never to write against the honor of womankind. The logical arguments and modernistic plots of Euripides' conceptual plays are contrasted with the female rituals and hymns to the symbolic gods of feasts and marriage. The old and the new are successfully harmonized in the society by the final agreement: that Euripides must not violate the norms of the conventional social mask. It seems that he will continue writing plays in the same vein; the women have neither punished him nor silenced him entirely. Their old habits and his new ideas adjust to one another socially in the eternal comic success.

JUSTICE AND PROSPERITY · *PLUTUS*

Athens in the years after her defeat, with the breakup of the old patterns of tribal and imperial life, felt increasingly the nonprobability of the human lot. Plato had discussed in the first two books of the *Republic* how the wicked prosper and the good too often languish in poverty and pain. In the defeated city this tragic awareness began to emerge in place of the older concept of exact justice for one's actions. Aristophanes in his last years abandoned strictly political themes, even in the abstract form of the *Ecclesiazusae,* to treat this general human issue from the comic point of view in the *Plutus* (388 B.C.).

Wealth (Plutus), the blind god, meets the Athenian citizen Chremylus and his slave Cario in the market place. When they find out who he is, they persuade him that they will heal his sight in order that he may mete out prosperity to the just alone. By this means the whole state will be wealthy, for all will become just in order to gain riches. In time the social ills of the city will be obliterated. Wealth says he has been blinded by Zeus so that he cannot distinguish between the just and the unjust. Chremylus soon convinces him that for the majority of men the probability of money means more than the wonder of religion. Even when they sacrifice to Zeus, it is usually to gain material advantage. Surely Wealth's power is greater than that of the king of the gods. One of Chremylus' fellow citizens, Blepsidemos (See-People), gets wind of the new arrival and searches out his friend. Meanwhile, Poverty, a dirty, ragged goddess, appears on the scene. When they explain to her the benefits that will accrue from the restored sight of Wealth, she replies in a parody of logic:

> *Why, if Wealth should allot himself equally out*
> > *(assume that his sight you restore),*
> *Then none would to science his talents devote*
> > *or practice a craft any more.*
> *Yet if science and art from the world should depart,*
> > *pray whom would you get for the future*
> *To build you a ship, or your leather to snip,*
> > *or to make you a wheel or a suture?*
> *Do you think that a man will be likely to tan,*
> > *or a smithy or laundry to keep,*

Or to break up the soil with his ploughshare, and toil,
the fruits of Demeter to reap.
If regardless of these he can dwell at his ease,
a life without labor enjoying?

Chremylus answers, as Praxagora does in her system, that the slaves will do all the work. When Poverty asks where one will get the slaves, Chremylus replies, "Buy them," completing the perfect circle of illogic. In spite of Poverty's arguments, he takes Wealth at night to the shrine of Aesclepius to be healed of his blindness. During the night the priest eats all the soup offerings and puts ointment on people's eyes. In this comic parody of religion, Chremylus frightens a woman sleeping nearby from stealing the soup by feigning with his fingers a sacred snake, and gobbles down all the soup himself. Yet the god does actually come with the two magic serpents and heals the eyes of Wealth. Wise Chremylus, having cured Wealth, handles appropriately all requests for money. An old lady comes in whose young gigolo has abandoned her since Wealth has been dwelling in Athens. Hermes arrives on the scene to say that the gods are starving for offerings, and Chremylus bargains for piety in return for the grant that Wealth will abide permanently in the Athenian treasury. Promising the old lady her gigolo that night for service in carrying pots of offerings, Chremylus succeeds in his plan, and all becomes prosperity and peace. The tension between the new abstract money (Wealth) and the old symbolic gods (Zeus) has again been resolved by the successful comic character.

Aristophanes, mirroring the rapid development of Greek culture itself, exemplifies in his dramas the whole gamut of a civilization from atavistic ritual patterns to the most advanced intellectual ideas. As a comic dramatist of the social and probable, he idealized the harmonious norms of the old aristocratic society at Athens, which lived its feudal life in the country guided by the religious ideals of its mores and the symbolic poets of its heroic past. The crux for the new Athenian empire he wrote about was the dilemma of democracy as highest individual development (wonderful,

Socratic-Platonic) and democracy as rabble (probable, Sophistic). The self-questioning of Socrates and other original conceptual thinkers threatened to cut the state off from the norms of the old traditions. But they also promised to redevelop the symbolic traditions by vigorous questioning. Aristophanes did not fully understand that the old tribal Athens, even without its barbarous practices, had disappeared for better or for worse. As he symbolically attacked in his social comedies the conceptual individualism of Euripides, Socrates, and Plato, so the normal Athenian citizen expelled the intellectuals who were their only hope.

Art changes nothing; it only explores meanings for the individual soul, which must will its own change through religion. Therein lies its inner wonderful success and its outward probable failure. So in his exploration of human nature versus conventions, city versus country, tradition versus intellectualism, Aristophanes failed to reform Athens but produced an eternally symbolic comedy of ideas.

MOLIERE
THE NEUROTIC DEVIATION OF THE BOURGEOIS

La parfaite raison fuit toute extrémité
Et veut que l'on soit sage avec sobriété.

Nothing in comedy is more removed from the boisterous rusticity of Aristophanes' symbolic clowns than the calm urbanity of the bourgeois characters in Molière. The seriousness in his plays approaches the ironic detachment of a probable modern novelist, like Flaubert or Thackeray. Whereas Aristophanes draws his subjects from politics and cultural history, Molière considers only the personal relations of social men in a bourgeois society. Aside from the broad development of individualism and commerce in the Renaissance and his own personal relations with Louis XIV, the history of his day has almost no meaning for his comedies. In discussing Aristophanes one must constantly rehearse year by year the events of the Peloponnesian War. But with Molière the policies of Mazarin, Colbert, and Fouquet, the revolution of the Fronde, the wars in Spain and Holland, the vacillations of Louis XIV, pass in another sphere from that of the plays. Though more than one pedantic French critic discusses these historical events at great length in writing on Molière, in order to understand him one should properly concern oneself not with history but with social psychology. The sphere of action in his plays is family, not state; the régime is reflected only in the prosperity or affectation of the characters.

The probable activities of the bourgeois are fit subjects for comedy, and in no author are the social manners of that class more deeply explored than in Molière. His dramas, consistent with the social, probable nature of comedy, proceed from a philosophy of the mean; but the fact that they were written in a civilization whose official religion is one of extreme has led many critics into discussing his ethos from the wrong point of view. To consider social comedy in the light of the ethical code proper to tragedy produces at best distortion and at worst error. It matters little that Brunetière calls him, with Faguet, a complete hedonist, or that Sainte-Beuve considers him religious. Any description of Molière's comedy should proceed from the bourgeois code of best social policy, not the Christian system of good and evil.

AGAMEMNON AND PASSIVE HYBRIS

The hybris of the great tragic hero is active. Fully confident of his powers, the individual hero acts in his cosmos, society, in an excess of pride that causes his own downfall. He feels that his individuality cannot be conquered; therefore like a god he can will the perfection of his own action. But in denying man's limitation, he is brought by excess of egotism to humility, to the overpowering knowledge of his own tragic flaw. The excess of his action and the darkness of his motivation bring an excess of passive suffering; it is the causal bond between the flaw and the suffering which wakes him to the knowledge of his limitation as a man. The glorious Achilles of the pure-action deed at the start of the *Iliad* becomes the self-conscious Achilles at the end, by realizing that society (therefore ultimately himself) suffers from his egotistical withdrawal. Oedipus the self-confident intellectual king becomes Oedipus the humble religious prophet. Brutus, Lear, Othello—all are proud, all turn inward after their proud action to a knowledge of their own sin. The hybris of the tragic hero is active, and must be cured by passive suffering. His error is the attempt to achieve godhead, an attempt at which man must always fail.

In contrast to this is the passive hybris of the bourgeois hero. Where Achilles ventures into the wonder of his action, the bourgeois hero trembles passively and maneuvers industriously in the probable to see that fate does not cheat him. He wants to make sure that when he puts a nickel into the slot machine of the cosmos he gets back a full nickel's worth, even if he has to pound the machine violently. This pounding of the machine is not to be confused with active hybris; the tragic hero actively creates his fate, whereas the bourgeois hero in passive hybris tries to adjust it to equitable dealing.

The flaw of passive hybris is denial of the problem of pain. Men are not rewarded in this world according to their deserts; he who thinks otherwise risks incurring unexpected woe. As the hero of active hybris destroys himself by proud action, the hero of passive hybris warps his personality in the effort to keep absolute justice in exchanges between himself and the cosmos. One cannot thus force the gods; when Agamemnon in passive hybris will use the iron rule of his kingly power to keep his bargain with the cosmos fair, he nevertheless pays the added price of becoming a bad king, hated by his society. He thinks when the cosmos offers him one unit for two, he can force it to give two for two. He does not realize that his impious denial of the problem of pain makes the exchange two plus warping of the personality, for two. In active hybris egotism seeks its own death; in passive hybris the jealous searcher for justice unwittingly makes injustice even greater by sacrificing his personality for equity in material exchanges.

Agamemnon is typical in his passive hybris. Like the bourgeois, he strives industriously to keep fate from cheating him. Though his share of plunder as king always exceeds that of his heroes, he still hovers nervously over that share, and grows indignant if anyone diminishes it in any way. Thersites rightly accuses him of being greedy over spoil. Though he has an abundance of concubines, when one is taken from him to appease Apollo he must make up for it by depriving Achilles of his. And he will despoil "you, or Ajax, or Odysseus" if need be.

In the *Iliad* the situation is ideal for the clash of the active hybris of Achilles with the passive hybris of Agamemnon. If Achilles were king, he would never have any trouble; he would simply fight well and lead passably. If Agamemnon were just another noble, he would not from Homer's point of view be a tragic character, but merely a querulous grumbler like Thersites. For Agamemnon and Thersites are very much alike; it is only the social rank which makes the difference between passive hybris as tragedy for one and incident for the other. A later age could make a tragic character out of a Thersites, but by exploring the inner soul rather than the outer actions. For Homer, as the official poet of an aristocracy, the hero of passive hybris, to develop tragically, must be placed as king in the heart of the social body.

The error of active hybris is the desire for godhead; that of passive hybris, the denial of the problem of pain. The one is individual and wonderful in terms of the soul's good and evil; the other, probable and social in terms of pleasure and pain. Oedipus helped the state by destroying the Sphinx, and the members of his society deliberately put his sin out of their minds till they began to suffer. Society loves Oedipus, no matter how spotted his individual soul, because he performs glorious deeds which are a source of its admiration and benefit. Because their social function is productive, society always embraces its Machiavellis; but it hates the capitalists whose passive hybris amasses wealth at its expense. While Achilles makes life more secure, Agamemnon threatens freedom of action. Paradoxically, the individual sin of active hybris may produce social benefit, while the social sin of passive hybris incurs individual pain. The aristocratic hero errs actively by blackening his soul; the bourgeois hero errs passively by making himself abnormal in social relationships.

Tragedies of passive hybris, such as the *Agamemnon* of Aeschylus, increase with the growth of an acquisitive mercantile society. The rise of individualism and commercial values during the Renaissance foreshadowed the passive hybris which is the basic neurosis of bourgeois man in society. Such a character is Angelo in *Measure for Measure,* whose suppression of normal passion into business life completely disrupts his personality. All the tragic heroes of Ibsen and Strindberg are passive in hybris, not active. Even the Master Builder really desires fame and love, not godhead; the active hybris Ibsen strives for so desperately in this play is passive in spite of all he can do.

THE BOURGEOIS AND THE ABNORMALITY OF CHANGE OF CLASS

The active hybris of the aristocrat fails in death. The passive hybris of the bourgeois makes him more unhappy as he becomes more asocial. Only in the accumulation of money, mere quantitative gain, can the bourgeois find an outlet for his anxiety drive toward security and love. If his neurosis seeks solution in any other way, he must either transform himself or fail. So in *Le Bourgeois Gentilhomme,* Monsieur Jourdain, who searches for the nonprobability of aristocracy, only brings violence on himself by disrupting the norms of his bourgeois life. Monsieur Jourdain is determined to make himself a gentleman in spite of his stolid success as a merchant. In middle age, with a marriagable daughter, he dresses himself in finery, hires dancing, fencing, and music teachers, and undertakes lessons with a philosopher—all in an effort to cultivate himself. He lavishes his money in the attempt to court the widowed marquise, Dorimène. Against the bourgeois common sense of his wife, he refuses his daughter Lucille to her beloved Cléonte when Cléonte confesses honestly that he is not an aristocrat. He wants to marry her to an aristocrat, if possible to his new friend, the impecunious count Dorante.

But the attempt to rise from the norms of his bourgeois life creates only pain for him. Jourdain becomes a laughingstock to his neighbors, and even to the attendants he has hired to dress and instruct him in aristocratic fashion. The penniless Dorante drains him of thousands; while supposedly pressing Jourdain's suit with Dorimène, he is actually pressing his own. In the secret banquet Jourdain holds for Dorante and Dorimène, he unwittingly becomes the more their laughingstock the more he tries to pay aristocratic court to Dorimène. As her husband becomes the complete fool, Madame Jourdain breaks in on the scene and scolds him. Meanwhile Lucille languishes to become the wife of Cléonte, but she stands checked in this normal desire by the abnormal concern of her father for his own selfish schemes. At last, however, love conquers all in the traditional comic success as Cléonte enters, disguised as an aristocratic Turk (the wonderful stranger); Jourdain readily consents to marry his daughter to a foreign nobleman, and in a final ballet the two are united.

Though this play leaves unresolved the strings of its entanglements, we assume that Monsieur Jourdain returns to the norms of his bourgeois life. The abnormal selfishness of his search for aristocracy has been thwarted by the normal self-interest of the rest of society: Dorante and Dorimène, who are probably matched to each other; Cléonte and Lucille, whose similarity in age and social station makes their marriage probable; and the common sense of his wife, who is shocked at the talk that is circulating about her family. Nothing to excess; only in the norms of social life does joy exist. Where Monsieur Jourdain expects the abnormal joy of aristocracy, he finds only the pain of failure in departing from the probability of his class.

In *George Dandin,* a rich peasant has married out of his station into a poor aristocratic family. There can be no pleasurable reward when the norms have been so transgressed, and the poor fellow, unable to please his wife because of his boorish manners, sees cuckoldry imminent. Despite the fact that he intercepts messages between the courtier Clitandre and his wife Angélique, tells her parents about it, and even catches her in the act, the duplicity of her diplomatic action and her parents' shocked respectability combine to make poor George Dandin, not his wife, the one who is blamed. On one occasion he is forced to apologize to his wife's seducer, and at the end of the play, the morning after he has been cuckolded, he is made to kneel and beg his wife's forgiveness. Even at the beginning of the play he says of his condition:

> Mon mariage est une leçon bien parlante à tous les paysans qui veulent s'élever au-dessus de leur condition, et s'allier, comme j'ai fait, à la maison d'un gentilhomme. . . . C'est notre bien seul qu'ils épousent: et j'aurois bien mieux fait, toute riche que je suis, de m'allier en bonne et franche paysannerie, que de prendre une femme qui se tient au-dessus de moi. . . . George Dandin, George Dandin! Vous avez fait une sottise. . . .

The social-climbing maidens Madelon and Cathos in *Les Précieuses Ridicules* find that life is much more probable and solid than they would have it. They are fascinated by the airy nonprobable fancies of the long romantic novels by the Scudéries and d'Urfé. The aristocratic social intercourse of the salons of the *précieuses* seems to them far more real than the blind conventions of bourgeois life. They desire the wonder of romance and perpetual courtship, not the probability of marriage and sex; Madelon says to her father Gorgibus:

> Mon Dieu! que si tout le monde vous ressembloit, un roman seroit bientôt fini! La belle chose que ce seroit si d'abord Cyrus épousoit Mandane, et qu'Aronce de plain-pied fut marié à Clélie!

She would violate social economy by prolonging courtship.

Unable to look life in the face, Madelon and Cathos reject honest suitors of their own class, La Grange and du Croisy. Marriage must be horrible; how could a woman endure to sleep beside a man *"vraiment nu"*? But their own lack of experience in the manners of the *précieuses* soon becomes evident. Decked in the paints and laces of the frivolous aristocracy they imitate, they easily fall prey to the deceptions of the valets of La Grange and du Croisy, who have been disguised as noblemen by their masters

92

for revenge on the two girls. The grossness of the girls surpasses that of the valets, till one of the latter wants to undress to show the wounds he supposedly incurred in battle. Only when they learn that they are being courted by servants do they come to their senses. Their own folly becomes clear and at the end of the play they are covered with shame. Throughout the play the manners of preciosity are revealed to be as blindly conventional as the bourgeois conventions which the two girls criticize so haughtily. And one assumes that the greater practicality of those norms, forced on the girls by society in the form of their suitors, will eventually bring Madelon and Cathos back to social probability.

Women so intent on the shallow search for the wonderful that they cannot stomach the probable are also represented in *Les Femmes Savantes*. In this play, Chrysale, *"bon bourgeois,"* his daughter Henriette, and his brother Ariste all desire to live a normal life by bourgeois common sense, whereas Chrysale's wife Philaminte, her sister-in-law Bélise, and her daughter Armande are enticed by the fashionable intellectualism of the literary coteries and their decadent aristocrats. When Henriette expresses her wish to marry the honest suitor Clitandre, her sister Armande recoils at the vulgarity of the plan. Like Madelon and Cathos in *Les Précieuses Ridicules,* she wants the wonder of courtship, not the probability of marriage "and all that it implies":

> Laissez aux gens grossiers, aux personnes vulgaires
> Les bas amusements de ces sortes d'affaires. . . .
> A de plus hauts objets élevez vos désirs,
> Et, traitant de mépris les sens et la matière,
> A l'esprit, comme nous, donnez-vous tout entière.
> Vous avez notre mère en exemple à vos yeux
> Que du nom de savante on honore en tous lieux:
> Tâchez, ainsi que moi, de vous montrer sa fille;
> Aspirez aux clartés qui sont dans la famille,
> Et vous rendez sensible aux charmantes douceurs
> Que l'amour de l'étude épanche dans les coeurs.
> Loin d'être aux lois d'un homme en esclave asservie,
> Mariez-vous, ma soeur, à la philosophie.

Their mother Philaminte wants to marry Henriette (not Armande!) not to the sensible Clitandre but to the foppish pedant Trissotin. But society, in the form of his brother Ariste, brings their father Chrysale to the common-sense intention of ruling in his own household. As he asserts himself toward the end of the play, it is announced that Madame by her devotion to spiritual matters alone has lost several thousands in law suits. As in *Madame Bovary*, the pseudointellectual searcher for the wonderful is driven outside the norm by the disruption of family life and the loss of money. When financial failure is announced, the pedant Trissotin shows his true colors by withdrawing his suit of marriage. His attraction for Henriette has not been purely spiritual, nor even the physical passion which he confesses in dialogue with her. He is simply a social climber and financial opportunist. His poetry, like that of Bunthorne in *Patience*, becomes from the probable point of view a vain and selfish pose. But Clitandre is still willing to marry Henriette; he insists on standing by her in her new poverty. The bourgeois husband reënters the norms by establishing himself in his rightful position as master of the household, and the young bourgeois couple will preserve those norms with their healthy marriage. But the airy intellectuality of the savants, who try to rise from their bourgeois condition, dissolves itself in sterility and petty spite.

THE ANXIETY OF SEARCH FOR MONEY · *L'AVARE*

The aristocratic hero desires the wonderful change of adventure and discovery; the bourgeois wants the probable stability of security. Where the searcher wishes to extend his cosmos, the bourgeois wants to cement it into place. Anxiety neurosis, the characteristic malaise of a commercial civilization, drives the bourgeois toward security and love, the physical and emotional guarantees against destitution, pariahism, and hostility. Material property of any sort, especially money, seems to the anxious bourgeois the surest means of achieving safety; he strives for money with all his time and effort. But the cosmos of society takes revenge for this passive hybris, and the bourgeois becomes abnormal in personality to the degree to which he sacrifices himself to gain wealth. Harpagon in Molière's *L'Avare* by his abnormal greed to get money from the rest of society brings only pain on himself and his family. His daughter Elise loves Valère, an honest young man of average means; Harpagon in his miserliness wants selfishly to marry her to the old Anselme, who is willing to take her without dowry. The sixty-year-old Harpagon, however, is willing to spend some of his money on himself alone, in seeking to marry the luscious young widow Mariane. He blindly and selfishly tries to check his son Cléante's normal love for Mariane in order to satisfy his own abnormal desires. But by his very anxiety for security and love he destroys his chances to gain them. Everybody hates him—his children, his servants, all who have dealings with him. In his hybris he would transform the normality of his family, the happiness of his children, and ultimately his own stability, into cold cash.

The resources of society, however, are greater than those of any individual who tries to wrest life into a position around his own ego. Harpagon finds that the chest of money which (symbolically) he buried in his garden, has been stolen. He suspects everybody, including those who are closest to him. A misunderstanding between himself and Valère, who has entered Harpagon's domestic service to win Elise, produces a long dialogue wherein the term "little treasure" is taken in the sense of love by Valère and money by Harpagon. At length old Anselme turns out to be the long-lost father of his shipwrecked children Valère and Mariane, who then first discover that they are brother and sister. Since Anselme is wealthy and will stand all expenses, Harpagon consents that Elise should marry Valère. Then Cléante implies that he himself has stolen the casket and that his father will get it back only if Cléante is allowed to marry Mariane. All the normal people who desire to live a sociable bourgeois life succeed at the end of the play. Only old Harpagon, still cherishing his miserliness, remains selfish and alone. Deaf actually to the words and symbolically to the emotions of those around him, his last words in the play express gladness at recovery of his treasure. Set in his ways, he does not know that his delight implies disaster, and that what he selfishly sacrifices for money can be his only source of delight. The abnormal bourgeois is expelled/expels himself from society in profound failure, while those who remain in the norms of "nothing to excess" achieve the probability of success.

ABNORMAL ATTITUDES TOWARD LOVE, COURTSHIP AND MARRIAGE

Sex is the most social and probable of all activities. And marriage is the probable culmination of all the mental overtures to love, which on the animal (rational, probable) level are nothing more than enticements to prolong the race. The success of normality and the failure of abnormality are nowhere so evident as in the attraction of women toward men. "No decent woman" will have the pariah, whereas the pure-action hero is crowned with the success of winning the most beautiful partner; none but the brave deserves the fair. Molière usually avoids the extremes of aristocracy and pariahism, the love among which classes could occupy the greater attention of Shakespeare and Dostoievsky; his normal ideal is the courtship of average bourgeois men with average bourgeois women. Since love of the opposite sex is socially the greatest single factor in one's ego, those who are plagued like Harpagon with abnormal anxiety strive abnormally to win and preserve love. The normal bourgeois lives in peace with his wife, but the anxious bourgeois sees always before his eyes the disgrace (insecurity/hatred) of cuckoldry.

The theme of cuckoldry—basic to all comedy—is first developed only farcically by Molière in early plays like *Le Cocu Imaginaire*. Later his personal marital troubles led him to give it a profound basis in the anxiety of the abnormal bourgeois like himself.

In *L'Ecole des Maris,* Ariste, courting his ward Léonor, is able to surmount the fact that he is middle-aged by unusual diplomacy and wisdom. His younger brother Sganarelle should normally be able to win his own ward Isabelle as wife; but his abnormal egotism, posing as idealism and renunciation of worldly ways, induces him to lock her up so that no suitors can get at her. He treats her masteringly and harshly, whereas Ariste treats Léonor with consummate gentleness. For this, Sganarelle, who in his ego-flaunting constantly reminds his brother of advancing age, warns Ariste that he will be made a cuckold if he is not more careful. Meanwhile, the normal young bourgeois Valère is able to make overtures to Isabelle, in spite of Sganarelle's surveillance over her. As the effect of egotism (aversion) is the opposite of what the egotist desires (affection), so Sganarelle's very struggles against Valère are symbolically turned into favor for that normal lover. He unwittingly becomes the intermediary between Valère and Isabelle; while he thinks he is vanquishing Valère, he is actually helping him. In a scene of boastful triumph in which he thinks he is most lording it over Valère, he is actually being most greatly duped. At last Isabelle, who learns with horror that Sganarelle intends to marry her the next day, tells him that her sister Léonor is herself involved with Valère and wishes to marry him secretly that night under the name of Isabelle. Sganarelle's selfish desire to see his older brother duped induces him to aid in the scheme which will bring about his own disgrace. When the normal marriage takes place, and the ruse has been openly announced, the enraged and disgraced Sganarelle blows up at the complete frustration of all his plans. He bursts violently out of the room in which the loving couples Valère-Isabelle and Ariste-Léonor are gathered in their normal social success. The diplomatic sagacity of Ariste has conquered, as was probable, the selfish, idealistic schemes of Sganarelle. At the end he renounces women and the world entirely as he rages out of the scene:

> Malheureux qui se fie à femme après cela!
> La meilleure est toujours en malice féconde;
> C'est un sexe engendré pour damner tout le monde.
> J'y renonce à jamais, à ce sexe trompeur,
> Et je le donne tout au diable de bon coeur.

So the normal characters will produce offspring to preserve the patterns of society intact, while the abnormal individualist, bourgeois or pariah, will die in sterility.

The play of the following year presents the foiled lover much more sympathetically. In L'Ecole des Femmes the position of the old jealous lover, Arnolphe, is as good as it possibly could be. He has been able to raise Agnès, the object of his love, in complete innocence from childhood (the dream of every old bachelor, as one critic says) under the care of two trusty peasants. Every care is taken to raise her as the wife of "Monsieur *de la* Souche" as Arnolphe fancies himself (assuming aristocracy and avoiding the name of St. Arnolphe, the patron saint of cuckolds). When he leaves town for a short time, Agnès quite openly and innocently comes under the influence of the young lover Horace, a friend of Arnolphe's. Since all the latter's relationships with Agnès are under a pseudonym, Horace does not know that Arnolphe is acquainted with his beloved and takes him as a confidant. Thinking Arnolphe his best friend, he tells him in great detail every stratagem he uses against "the old fool" and reads him every letter. Further, Agnès herself who has been raised to complete honesty, is openly frank with Arnolphe in everything. At last, Horace even hands Agnès over to Arnolphe in his house to keep her for him till he can marry her. But these advantages of Arnolphe's, great as they are, are merely surface detail compared to the life forces of nature which will destroy all planned schemes, such as the abnormal training of Agnès, to bring about a normal marriage. The force of life is too great, no matter how predictable its events may be, for old Arnolphe to disturb its norms by rearranging them around his own desires. Again at the end of the play the young girl marries the young man and Arnolphe storms out aghast. The abnormal suspicion of cuckoldry and the selfishness of desiring to marry one of a younger generation must end in disappointment and failure.

In *Le Mariage Forcé,* Sganarelle in his fifty-third year joyously plans to marry the young Dorimène. Everything seems all right, till he overhears her say to her lover Lycaste that she expects the old man to die before long, and then she will marry the younger lover. Dorimène herself is abnormally anxious to leave a household tyrannized by her father, but even so, Sganarelle must make up for the abnormality of the gap between their ages by allowing her abnormal luxury and freedom. He finds out too late, because he is forced into the marriage by her brother, who threatens him with a duel if he withdraws. Blindness at the beginning of the relationship will cost him pain; his abnormal selfishness brings its reward of abnormal suffering, even when he is prepared to correct himself.

Nature herself preserves the norms of life; in Homer even the gods are subject to fate. In the *Amphitryon* while the general for whom the play is named is away at battle, Jupiter seduces his wife Alcmène. Still, at the end of the play when his abnormal enjoyment is over, he joins the pair in a resumption of normal marriage ties. The child Hercules will be the issue of the adulterous act, but the norms of marriage still remain inviolate. The anxious bourgeois who tries to flout these norms brings on his own head the effects of his action. Resilient society returns to him the blow he tries to give it. All is probable, and preëminently so in sex, the great social probability of courtship and marriage. The egotism/death wish of courtly love, which de Rougemont traces in aristocratic French literature from Chrétien de Troyes through Racine, finds no expression in the bourgeois comedy of Molière. He sees all search in love, save for normal marriage, as one of the above-mentioned errors, or Don Juanism.

Don Juan is the most religious of Molière's plays, though it is still told from the point of view of the social and probable. It may be that the damnation of Don Juan at the end of the play reflects his own chagrin against the courtiers who were seducing the attentions of his coquettish wife Armande. At any rate, the jolliness—which sometimes verges on cruelty—of the other plays gives way in *Don Juan* to a sardonic grimness.

Don Juan is an egotistic searcher for the nonprobable in sex. A master of sophistry and Machiavellian diplomacy, he gloats diabolically over his success at conquest. That this egotism of the individual conquering society implies the tragic desire to be a god is expressed only negatively in Don Juan's atheism and his mockery of the will of heaven. While the Don is utterly self-confident in his amoralism, his vacillating servant Sganarelle is perpetually troubled in conscience. But his religion will not master the power of habit, the wages, and the ego-satisfaction gained from serving Don Juan. He stays on in the Don's service as the butt of his attacks against religion.

Molière's plot is nearly identical with that of Mozart's opera. As the play opens, Don Juan has abandoned Done Elvire, whom he had seduced from a convent to marry. He will not be confined within four walls, but will conquer the earth woman by woman. At the moment he is attracted by the young peasant girl, Charlotte, who is engaged to Pierrot, and Mathurine, another peasant girl whom he has already promised to marry. In the cleverness of his diplomacy he holds forth to these poor girls the wonder of change in social station from plebeian maidenhood to marriage with an aristocrat. In spite of his cleverness and mastery, society begins to defeat Don Juan in the form of Done Elvire's two brothers, Don Alonse and Don Carlos, who pursue him to revenge the seduction of their sister. But Don Juan saves Don Carlos' life from threatening robbers, and escapes being killed at the hands of the brothers by neatly playing off the convention of duty toward him who saves your life against the convention of killing your sister's seducer. In a scene just before this, Don Juan encounters a religious mendicant in the forest, taunts him with his probable lack of prosperity in the face of his continual wonderful prayers, and finally tempts him with a gold coin to blaspheme. When the beggar refuses, the Don throws him the coin anyway with a supercilious gesture.

The Christian unselfishness of Done Elvire's conjugal love makes her renounce Don Juan for the convent, yet urge him to repent and seek his salvation. His old father Don Louis is brokenhearted at his son's blackness; he tells him that aristocracy comes not from birth or property, but from actions. All through the play Don Juan mocks the will of heaven in his self-sufficiency. As in the opera, he invites to dinner the statue of the old man he had murdered some months before and remains true to his promise when the statue supernaturally keeps the engagement. The morning after the statue leaves, he tells his father that he renounces his old ways. The old man goes away delighted, to tell his wife the good news. But it turns out that the Don has said even this just as a ruse, and he uses it again to dupe Don Carlos. He says his repentance leads him to renounce all his old sinful ways, that he renounces the world—including a wife—for a religious life. Surely this does not mean that a wife's agreement is against the will of God, says Don Carlos. Not at all, says Don Juan; Done Elvire has taken exactly the same course by renouncing me, and I must do what heaven wills. A phantom of Justice fails to make him repent; he merely thrusts his sword at her to see if she is body or spirit. At last the statue comes back according to his word, and offers the Don his hand. In his self-confident show of bravery, Don Juan accepts, and is burned away to hell by an invisible fire. At the end the repentant Sganarelle reflects on the social disruption caused by the selfish individualism of the Don, and repents of his own service to him:

> Ah mes gages! mes gages! Voilà, par sa mort, un chacun satisfait. Ciel offensé, lois violées, filles séduites, familles deshonorées, parents outragés, femmes mises à mal, maris poussés à bout, tout le monde est content; il n'y a que moi seul de malheureux. Mes gages, mes gages, mes gages!

Everybody else has been the victim of deceit; Sganarelle alone has had a hand in Don Juan's sins. The ambiguity of "gages" (money wages/wages of sin) expresses the ambiguity of Sganarelle's service for benefit of pay/revulsion at the Don's irreligion.

Don Juan is not a tragedy, but a serious comedy. For the viewpoint, still social and probable, is that of a religion which has enshrined the honest habits of a people, marriage, and the family. There is no paradox of motivation, as in tragedy; Don Juan completely wills his damnation and his character is utterly black. Being wonderful, he is able to stir the normal woman into sin; but only for a short, nonprobable period of time. In the emergence of events the devil and his agent are vanquished and banished from the earth; their disruption of sexual norms is healed by the goodness of probable, natural society.

RELIGION AND THE HYPOCRITE · TARTUFFE

One year before writing Don Juan, Molière dramatized another irreligious abnormality in Tartuffe, the hypocrite whose complete air of virtue takes in all who are unaware, including himself. Orgon, a wealthy Parisian bourgeois, enamored of Tartuffe's steadfast praying and sober demeanor, has introduced him into his own home and favors him above even the members of his own family. Only Orgon's prudish mother, Madame

Pernelle, is also taken in by the devout and unctuous hypocrite; the normal members of society who are not so innocent as Orgon or so frigid as his mother see through him immediately. The pert Dorine, a servant girl with rough common sense, continually makes quips against him. Damis, Orgon's son, and Elmire, his second wife, soberly try to dissuade the head of their family from his infatuation. The very apostle of common sense in the family is Cléante, brother-in-law of Orgon, who draws from his pure-action knowledge of bourgeois character to analyze Tartuffe:

> Et comme on ne voit pas qu'où l'honneur les conduit,
> Les vrais braves soient ceux qui font beaucoup de bruit,
> Les bons et vrais dévots, qu'on doit suivre à la trace
> Ne sont pas ceux aussi qui font tant de grimace.
> Eh quoi! vous ne ferez nulle distinction
> Entre l'hypocrisie et la dévotion?

In his excess of innocence, and duped by Tartuffe's excess of selfishness, Orgon forces his family from the norms of bourgeois life. He wants to marry his young daughter Mariane to the old hypocrite, when she is clearly in love with the honest young bourgeois Valère.

The disintegration of the family under the excess of its father is shown on the stage for two acts before Tartuffe enters. In the third act, Orgon's wife, whom he has neglected for the hypocrite, is left alone with Tartuffe, who tries, still in the smug oiliness of his religion, to seduce her. "Ah, pour être dévot, je n'en suis pas moins homme!" he says. Elmire grows indignant. Her stepson, Damis, Orgon's son by a previous marriage, has overheard the whole scene. But when Damis insists against Tartuffe in the ensuing scene, Orgon is so sure of the hypocrite's virtue that he evicts Damis from the house and deprives him of his patrimony in favor of Tartuffe.

At last Elmire persuades Orgon to hide under a table and listen to Tartuffe's words of seduction. After a long dialogue with her, the hypocrite tells Orgon's wife what a duped fool her husband is. Orgon, outraged by the scoundrel, denounces Tartuffe on the spot and orders him out of the house. But he has signed all his property over to Tartuffe, and the hypocrite says he will keep it all to use it for the good of the church. Soon thereafter a police agent, as unctuously servile as Tartuffe is hypocritical, tells the family that they must abandon their house in the morning. As they face pariahism, Valère, the newly accepted fiancé of Mariane, comes in with another officer to clear matters up in favor of Orgon. The prince of the land is a benevolent and wise ruler, he says, who lets nothing escape his view. Though Tartuffe has a legal right to the property, the common sense of normal honest usage declares that it should not be his. Further, the hypocrite, not Orgon, is packed off to prison for his earlier crimes. With the natural norms restored, the new family of the younger generation will be founded:

> Et par un doux hymen couronner en Valère
> La flamme d'un amant généreux et sincère.

In probable terms, when the member of a normal family goes to excess as did Orgon, he is drawn back to the norms by the magnetic pull of the social family. On the other hand, the diehard abnormal individualist ignores (or, like Tartuffe, seems without) social ties, and goes his own way in spite of everyone. To Molière in his Christian society, only the abnormal saint, like the mendicant in *Don Juan,* is justified in excessive individualism and withdrawal into the self. The chief targets of Molière are the abnormalities which mask any deep selfishness that threatens the rest of the society with harm and the character himself with anxious frustration. The principle of "nothing to excess" also includes religion, and the convent in Molière—as to the average Catholic family today— is a place with which rebellious daughters are threatened. The normal social family does not want to see one of its members in the officially nonprobable position of orders.

Many of the abnormal characters suffer from the anxiety neurosis which ruthlessly tries to debase the ego of others in order to exalt its own. The abnormally jealous husband in Molière is always eager to see someone else made a cuckold. Nature takes care of itself in the supremacy and health of its norms; only the man driven by anxiety broods over money, love, social position—even honesty. Religion, the refuge of Tartuffe and

103

temporarily the ruse of Don Juan, can allow the vice of selfishness to masquerade as the virtue of altruism—but only for a time, because when the norms of this abnormal conduct emerge, they become predictable to some member of normal society. Tartuffe will be apprehended; the mendicant saint will probably be noticed briefly by the crowd, then passed by.

To Molière, bourgeois life was the honest, healthy ideal; to a tragic writer, the hypocrisy of Tartuffe would be less surprising than the openness and essential goodness of all the normal characters in the play. Dostoievsky, even Zola, would not have them so.

THE FOOLISH PEDANT AND THE UNSCRUPULOUS DOCTOR

The sterile intellectual arguments in *Les Précieuses Ridicules* contrast with the normal bourgeois diplomacy of the character who knows how to live sanely. For the blindest selfishness of all is to establish one's life on the false norms of books and Aristotelian rationalism rather than on the natural experience of emerging norms in life. Pancrace and Marthurius, the learned philosophers in *Le Mariage Forcé,* ridiculously argue about substance, accidence, and being when asked questions about a choice in love. To comedy, the more philosophic ideas become abstract, the more they are detached from nature. The norms of nature are healthy, but those of a manmade rational pattern contain only the disguise for individual selfishness and vanity. In *Le Bourgeois Gentilhomme,* the teacher of philosophy, who violates the probable laws of economy by speculating endlessly about trivia, becomes enraged with the dancing master and the music teacher when they suggest that their disciplines are as dignified (full of ego-satisfaction) as his. Such selfish doctors, clad in the false security of their pedantry, can only obscure the all-healing work of nature's norms. They consider themselves superior to the bourgeois, but actually, says comedy, their scraps of book learning are wretched in comparison with his pure-action wisdom. In vain the bores in *Les Fâcheux*—the singer, the hunter, the card player, the philosophers of love—attempt to interrupt the frantic lover who is searching for his beloved.

The anxiety of the bourgeois for security in love, money, and social standing can become abnormal and drive him into pariahism. The greatest anxiety of all attaches to security from death, the irrevocable act of his cosmos on man. Anxiety for health is the yearning to escape the insecurity of man's lot on earth; sooner or later every man who holds passive hybris in something else is attacked by hypochondria. In this neurosis the unscrupulous doctor finds ample scope for exploitation, and he does not hesitate to milk the hypochondriac. As Monsieur Filerin says in *L'Amour Médecin:*

> Le plus grand foible des hommes, c'est l'amour qu'ils ont pour la vie; et nous en profitons, nous autres, par notre pompeux galimatias, et savons prendre nos avantages de cette vénération que la peur de mourir leur donne pour notre métier.

In Molière's last play, *Le Malade Imaginaire,* Argan is a prey to the doctors, who stuff him with medicines and empty his purse. Again the abormality of the anxious bourgeois threatens the normal success of his family. He wants to will his property to his second wife, Béline, a treacherous and adulterous legacy hunter, because she pampers his hypochondria, and only the norms of the law in its wise pure-action experience prevent him from doing so. Further, he will marry his daughter Angélique to the young prig, Thomas Diafoirus, a promising medical pedant but insufferable person.

Argan's family pulls him out of the mess. Since he refuses to listen to sound advice, his brother Béralde and the sage little servant, Toinette, disguise the latter as a doctor to advise Argan. He consents to allow Cléante, a normal bourgeois whom she loves, to marry Angélique, if he will become a doctor; but at Toinette's persuasion decides to become a doctor himself! Society will indulge him in his foibles by countering his hypochondriac abnormality with its symbolic opposite, medical pedantry. The play ends in a burlesque ballet of Argan's dog-Latin doctoral examination by the medical faculty.

Contrasting with Argan's artificial room with its medicaments are the natural pastoral ballets, where the shepherds on the countryside dance in the health of their normal life. The abnormal concern for avoiding death only wastes Argan's fortunes; he should live like the average man under the care of the greatest healer, the living norms of nature, against which all pedantry is foolishness. As the young shepherdess says to the doctor at the beginning of this play:

> *Votre plus haut savoir n'est que pure chimère,*
> *Vains et peu sages médecines;*
> *Vous ne pouvez guerir, par vos grands mots latins,*
> *La douleur qui me désespère:*
> *Votre plus haut savoir n'est que pure chimère.*

Keen bourgeois like the lover of Valère in *L'Avare* soon see through a pedantic doctor's mask:

> Il faut demander un délai, et feindre quelque maladie.
> ELISE. Mais on découvrira la feinte, si l'on appelle des médecins.
> VALÈRE. Vous moquez-vous? Y connoissent-ils quelque chose? Allez, allez, vous pourrez avec eux avoir quel mal il vous plaira; ils vous trouveront des raisons pour vous dire d'où cela vient.

Though he has been only an assistant to a doctor, the woodcutter Sganarelle in *Le Médecin Malgré Lui* is able to feign all this sham successfully. His ignorance, like that of the professional doctor, easily hides itself behind irrelevant scraps of Latin and an authoritarian air. Forced into this disguise by his wife Mariane in revenge for the beatings he has given her, the pariah wastrel and drunkard Sganarelle is finally able to effect a cure for the muteness of Géronte's daughter Lucinde, not by medicine, but by love. He follows the hints of the wise nurse Jacqueline, and brings it about that Lucinde marry Léandre. There was nothing wrong with her but love. Love is the doctor, both in this play and in the similar *L'Amour Médecin*. The absurd theories of Sganarelle, with his bread dipped in wine and his pseudolearned ideas of the liver on the left side and the heart on the right ("nous avons changé tout cela"), are at best fruitless and at worst harmful. Love is no sickness; and even the illness of Argan seems to be merely abnormal concern for his own health.

It is easy to understand the selfishness of the jealous husband, the miser, the hypochondriac; but from the beginning of his career Molière also portrayed characters plagued with a more general incapacity. Lélie in *L'Etourdi* is unschooled in the ways of the world and must constantly be extricated from entangling situations by the diplomacy of his adroit valet, Mascarille. In his innocent idealism he can never see the social action which takes place around him. His judgment is perpetually too simple for events which the merest peasant would understand. So in *Le Dépit Amoureux* the honest Eraste is too jealous of his fiancée; but from other cause, it seems, than the jealousy of the husbands in later plays. He suffers not from their anxiety, but more generally from an incorrect attitude toward society. A similar jealousy is the subject of *Don Garcie de Navarre*, the play usually considered to be a rough draft of *Le Misanthrope*.

The excessive honesty and self-righteous bitterness of Alceste in *Le Misanthrope* cut him off from the affection and esteem of a society which he misprizes. At the beginning of the play he upbraids his normal friend, Philinte, for tact, which he calls pure servility:

> *Et vous me le traitez, à moi, d'indifferent!*
> *Morbleu! c'est une chose indigne, lâche, infame*
> *De s'abaisser ainsi jusqu' à trahir son âme;*
> *Et si, par un malheur, j'en avois fait autant,*
> *Je m'irois, de regret, pendre tout à l'instant.*

Alceste himself prefers death to insincerity. He pours his *saeva indignatio* on the human race for its norm of diplomacy.

Philinte, on the other hand, says that he and Alceste are like the two brothers in *L'Ecole des Maris,* where Ariste, the mild elder, presents a classic statement of probable wisdom to his jealous brother Sganarelle:

> *Mais je tiens qu'il est mal, sur quoi que l'on se fonde*
> *De fuir obstinement ce que suit tout le monde;*
> *Et qu'il vaut mieux souffrir d'être au nombre des fous,*
> *Que du sage parti se voir seul contre tous.*

The world will not change, says Philinte; you can only appear ridiculous to it if you refuse to accept it as it is and persist in the excess of frankness. So much the better! cries Alceste, who predicts the pain that must result from his action. But inconsistently with his principles, he himself is in love with the young widow Célimène; and he implies that it cannot be other than her pure-action coquetries which have infatuated him as a social man. The prude Arsinoe holds no attraction for him, nor does he deem the sincere Eliante, who admires him, other than a second choice.

Alceste's frankness has its effects, though he has the wisdom to predict them. When pressed for an honest verdict on Oronte's poem, he finally bursts out that it is bad and affected verse, incurring the invitation to a duel from the outraged man. His failure to negotiate in the courts makes him lose twenty thousand livres in a lawsuit. And his constant criticisms of Célimène's flirtations with other men anger her greatly. It is only after her wiles have been discovered to the four other lovers and they leave in a rage that she consents to choose Alceste alone. But the misanthrope, whose hatred for mankind is now complete, wants to retire to a country estate, far from all but his wife. The horrified young Célimène, whose greatest delight is social intercourse, refuses; Alceste turns to Eliante, who has clearly shown him the greatest favor all through the play. But her natural inclination for Alceste is not strong enough to endure the bleak abnormality he has resolved on, and she turns to the honest Philinte who has constantly been courting her. As Alceste's revulsion at the corruption of society becomes complete, so does his withdrawal into individuality:

> Trahi de toutes parts, accablé d'injustices,
> Je vais sortir d'un gouffre où triomphent les vices,
> Et chercher sur la terre un endroit écarté
> Où d'être homme d'honneur on ait la liberté.

One feels that he can only end in complete retreat or self-destruction, though the considerate Philinte concludes the play by answering that society will not let one of her honest members so destroy himself:

> Allons, madame, allons employer toute chose
> Pour rompre le dessein que son coeur se propose.

By exhibiting the most profound form of individual error, the renunciation of a corrupt society, Molière points to the conclusion that society's norms, however they may seem in the light of reason, afford the only means of success. Alceste does not make any of the more specific errors in Molière's plays; he is not abnormally jealous, watchful of his money, or concerned with his health. He is not innocent in the ways of the world, but understands perfectly the norms of social action. He owns a passive hybris not for specific material gain, like Agamemnon, or for love or avoidance of death, like the cuckolds and the hypochondriacs. His passive hybris is against the principle of the probable itself. His just, cold picture of society is the deepest and most general form of an error of which all the other cases are less profound examples; he refuses to accept the problem of pain, and in his demand for honesty and justice incurs his own failing frustration. Molière, who, like Shakespeare, experienced the humiliation of unhappy marriage and the pariahism of an actor's life, enters into the realm of Swiftian indignation and departs with the wisdom that therein lies failure. The sadness that surrounds Alceste is deeper and the laughter of Molière becomes muted to a grotesquerie. He is no fat buffoon, no pedant, no foolish egotist, no hypochondriac. All he says rings true, but his renunciations of what is false, as the action implies, must lead him to the sure severance of all social ties. From the social and probable point of view, one must accept the ways of the majority as they are, or one is doomed to failure. The error of logical reason as a guide to life is not presented in *Le Misanthrope* as humorous parody; it is followed to its implied conclusion and shown to involve frustration. The quotation used as a motto for this chapter is spoken by Philinte to Alceste. Its implications for these two characters mirror the whole position of comic thought.

THE FUNCTION OF COMEDY

Molière's view of art is presented partially in *L'Impromptu de Versailles,* in which the members of his troupe, juxtaposing third-personal and second-personal perspective, play themselves and discuss the technique of acting. Even fuller in aesthetic meaning is the other critical comedy written immediately before this, *La Critique de L'Ecole des Femmes,* which takes place symbolically in a social gathering at the house of Uranie, the normal bourgeois woman who likes Molière's comedy. The frigid and affected characters make objections to *L'Ecole des Femmes*. Elise, who, like the misanthrope, prefers solitude to society, finds it disgusting. Both the prudish *précieuse* Climène and the affected marquis are shocked by its outspokenness on sex. Lysidas, the poet who gives readings of his plays, complains that it violates the rules of Aristotle and Horace.

Against them Uranie, the well-balanced, unaffected woman in society and her cavalier friend Dorante defend *L'Ecole des Femmes* on principles which may fairly be considered those of Molière himself. The function of comedy is to adjust the manners of people to the healthy norms of nature, to avoid the excesses presented on the stage:

> Ces sortes de satires tombent directement sur les moeurs, et ne frappent les personnes que par réflexion. N'allons point nous appliquer nous-mêmes les traits d'une censure générale; et profitons de la leçon, si nous pouvons, *sans faire semblant qu'on parle à nous.* . . . Ce sont *miroirs publics,* où il ne faut jamais témoigner qu'on se voie.

In the social act of attending comedy, one preserves the mask of complete harmony—while noting on the stage one's own divergences from the norm, which can then be corrected to the norm.

Le bon sens should be the guide to merit, not the traditions of the ancients. Comedy represents men as they are *d'après nature.* Those who are normal, though with small excesses, will like Molière. But all abnormal people will fail to find him great literature. Finally the play closes with the comic viewpoint that the whole discussion is merely abstract, abnormal rationalism in comparison to the social meal which they are about to enjoy. Honest Dorante says:

> Ah! voila *justement* ce qu'il faut pour le dénouement que nous cherchions, et l'on ne peut rien trouver *de plus naturel.* On disputera fort et ferme de part et d'autre, comme nous avons fait, sans que personne se rende; un petit laquais viendra dire qu'on a servi, on se levera, et chacun ira souper.

Uranie remarks that the comedy could not have a better end.

110

The snobbish marquis complains in *La Critique* of the boorish taste of the pit, but the normal bourgeois reply to him that the opinion of the masses is just. If a sauce tastes good, if art pleases the majority, that is enough. The pure action of the masses' response is the aesthetic of the probable, hence of comedy. It matters not that the *Clouds* takes last place in the Athenian dramatic festival or that *Le Misanthrope*, Molière's most profound play, was almost a failure. The judgment of the society nevertheless means success in art as in action.

Molière's wisdom in the pure action of bourgeois life served him well with the stuff of his comedies. But in his position as manager it drew his time and attention from creation to manipulation. He succeeded so well in becoming popular—by his adroitness in business as much as by the merit of his comedies—that he eventually won the favor of Louis XIV. However lucrative and pleasant this favor may have been, the demands of the king for entertainment drained Molière's creative energies into aristocratic ballets, a genre ill suited to his gifts. Some comic writers like Chaucer and Shakespeare can write both bourgeois and aristocratic literature. The same pen that wrote the *Miller's Tale* could compose the aristocratic *Troilus and Cressida*. But Molière's talents, great as they were, held only for bourgeois comedy. As a writer of aristocratic ballets he was mediocre, and the time he spent on them is nearly wasted for literature.

More than one critic has seen in Molière a caged eagle, whose genius for one genre was sabotaged by the popular-courtly demand for another. But the very solidity of his bourgeois ideals and the keenness of his pure-action knowledge, which gave him the basis for producing the insights of his best comedies, implied a capacity for business management which in his time could only have brought him to the position in which he found himself. Character is the guiding spirit of a man; no managerial acumen, no great comedies. Every man is enmeshed in his environs; the weakness of seventeenth-century France must in terms of his own individuality become the weakness of any writer in the period. The cold pessimism of La Rochefoucauld, the airy escapism of Madame Guyon, the chaste tragic limitations of Racine, alike spring from the elaborate stasis of seventeenth-century aristocracy. Whether one is satirical, mystical, or idealistically moral, an attitude models itself on the milieu toward which one takes it. The blunt—and essentially equivalent—enthusiasm of king and pit was what Molière valued as a social comic writer.

Fortunately for his own dark voyage, the pain of Molière's personal life in his last ten years led him to deeper insights in his drama. The flirting of his young wife Armande and his own obscure illness both lacerated him and allowed him to explore the social meanings of marriage and medicine, his two most frequent subjects.

Transcending the boisterousness of Plautus, Italian farce, Rabelais— indeed, of nearly all previous comedy—he developed the philosophy of the mean in all its social implications; the selfish excesses of miserliness, hypochondria, marrying out of one's generation or one's social station, prudishness as an ego-defense against one's own lack of sexual attractiveness, finally the profound search of the soul for honesty, which brings the individual to despair in passive hybris toward his social cosmos. Though his point of view is social and probable, he is almost the only comic writer who is able to penetrate the neurosis of the failing individual. This understanding approaches the sadness of tragedy, and led Alfred de Musset to say of his dramas:

> *Quel grand et vrai savoir des choses de ce monde,*
> *Quelle mâle gaîté, si triste et si profonde,*
> *Que lorsqu' on vient d'en rire, on devrait en pleurer.*

GILBERT · DODGSON · BUTLER
IN NINETEENTH-CENTURY BRITAIN

How quaint the ways of Paradox!
At common sense she gaily mocks!

—THE PIRATES OF PENZANCE

When the new seriousness of the Industrial Revolution and the French Revolution had begun to subside into bourgeois probability, the non-probable tragedy of the Romantic poets was succeeded by the probability of comedy. Britain had traditionally taken the shocks of the new age in beefy vigor. The British Empire extended itself still more after the defeat of Napoleon and full acquisition of India. A stable, elaborate code of manners, in the pure action of politics and drawing-room etiquette, settled into the Victorian Age, a contrast with the social life of the eighteenth century which did not have to cope greatly with either the government of an empire or the lower classes. Along with the probability of empire, the rationales of symbolic logic were explored by British philosophers, Hamilton, Boole, Charles Dodgson, and later Russell and Whitehead. Utopian social rationalism and the progress of science were confused by the shallower nonprobable rebels against the pure-action empire; and are so confused by pseudo-intellectuals to this day.

The Empire under Queen Victoria was still royalist and aristocratic, though it had made valuable concessions to the working classes in voting laws and working conditions. While thousands of play-hardened, sporting, and presumably cultured diplomats rolled off the Eton-Harrow Oxford-Cambridge assembly line, the academic thinkers brooded over the meanings of the official church. All of them—Pusey, Ruskin, Manning, even Newman—were dominated by neurotic hesitation and the abnormal desire for respectability.

The two bugbears of this empire were the unnaturalness of its conventions and its exploitation of the lower classes. Artists who tried to conform deeply to those conventions became corrupt. Ruskin writhed in a sickish romanticism which prevented him from having intercourse with the woman who was eight years his wife; like Charles Dodgson and Ernest Dowson he had the habit of falling in love with ethereal young girls. William Morris and the pre-Raphaelites espoused a feeble medievalism as escapist as the Hellenism of their compatriots at the beginning of the century. The failure to face the implications of an artist's life in desiring to live as a respectable bourgeois while creating forced Matthew Arnold into school inspecting and Walter Pater into the academy. Tennyson

115

suppressed his coarse-grained masculinity for an elegant paleness which sapped his poems of their vitality. On all these tragic writers, in their attempt to be at one with bourgeois conventions and their failure to gain self-knowledge, lies the taint of shallowness. Even those like Charles Dodgson who were deeply kind and obsessively religious considered, as far as we can judge, only their shallower and more obvious sins, not the deep paradox of their own motivation. The wastes of Browning are as gray as the wastes of Shaw, and for the same reason: the mask of intellectualism hides their essential failure to come to grips with paradox. This is becoming obvious with Browning and will so for Shaw when another fifty years reveals the real shallowness of his eager rationalism, his bowelled Nietzsche, Wagner, and Ibsen, his Christ made rationalistically respectable to a liberal convention.

While these effete authors wove the traceries of their fancy, the dark, toil-grimed hordes of the lower classes threw the shadow of guilt over their private incomes and their padded, respectable individualism. Hopkins, who explored his own soul more deeply than any Englishman of his century, wrote to Bridges that the lower classes might justifiably destroy a culture which was produced by an élite that had plundered their labor. They would be wrong, said Hopkins, but their question is terrible and just. In his next letter to Bridges, however, he replies to that self-righteous bourgeois in a withdrawal and apology of his "red" talk. Cowardly as this retraction may seem to a modern liberal, the insight of Hopkins was keener, not to say more honest, than that of almost any other writer in Britain at the time. The lower classes made them all uneasy, but they all avoided the problem.

The comic writers discussed these problems with more realism than these poets and philosophers. In their queer probings, their neurotic failures, the strange tone of their vision of the golden mean, they produced an art which is more interesting and greater than that of their more serious successors, Shaw and Galsworthy. W. S. Gilbert, Lewis Carroll, and Samuel Butler are at once more colorful and deeper than Shaw, all of whose problems they foreshadow. English comedy had not been so fertile since the similar imperial expansion of the Elizabethan Age.

The conservativism of comedy is reflected in the comedy of Gilbert, which accepts without question, while it twits them, the social classes of Victorian England. In this comedy, romantic though it parodies romanticism, the bourgeois class of realistic Molière is neglected. The romanticized kings and queens of nonprobable space and time are the highest class: Kings Hildebrand and Gama in *Princess Ida,* the Mikado of Japan, the gods in *Thespis.* Next come the aristocrats in attendance on them: the Dukes in *Ruddigore* and *The Gondoliers,* noblemen in *The Sorcerer* and *Yeomen of the Guard.*

In these comedies aristocrats mingle with idyllic members of pastoral lower classes. As Empson shows in *Some Versions of Pastoral,* the aristocrat and the shepherd, the two ideal types of natural order, each borrow in pastoral the virtues of the other class; naturalness and elegance thereby become qualities of both. As in *A Winter's Tale* and *As You Like It,* the maid of aristocracy loves the humble pastoral swain, and the nonprobability of this is successfully solved by the surprise/omniscient revelation of the comic plot, which discovers that one or another is actually an aristocrat. As Florizel plays shepherd/is prince and Perdita lives shepherdess/is princess, so Luiz in *The Gondoliers,* who seems a mere attendant, turns out in a parody of the changeling child motif to be the real king of Barataria. Casilda's love for him is right after all; class will truly know class, and the born aristocrat will be revealed in the end so that all society may live harmoniously. The gondoliers, in mistaken identity, may actually take over the kingdom for a short nonprobable time. But their lack of pure-action experience in ruling makes them and their subjects miserable. They betray their own trade in the act of kingship and are happier as gondoliers married to plebeian maidens. Further, the Utopianism of their democratic monarchy violates the laws of probability; in making everybody a lord, they fail to meet the first condition of an aristocracy: that its numbers be nonprobable in proportion to the population. The plebeian/pariah actors in *Thespis* cannot manage Olympus as well as the gods did, however decrepit the gods may have become. Their own personal problems as bourgeois types symbolically conflict with their wonder-

117

ful functions as gods. Still, the wonderful duties of the gods are shown to be as probable as the business of a bourgeois, and the comic Olympus is run like a commercial house, with the trusted underling Mercury doing all the work:

> Up here it's simply contemptible. Now that you gods are too old for your work, you've made me the miserable drudge of Olympus—groom, valet, postman, butler, commissionaire, maid of all work, parish beadle, and original dustman. . . . I do everything and I'm nothing. I've made thunder for Jupiter, odes for Apollo, battles for Mars, and love for Venus. I've married couples for Hymen and divorced them for Cupid—and in return I get all the kicks while they pocket the halfpence.

Gilbert, in parody of romantic pastoral like the poems of Wordsworth and the novels of Scott, portrays rural people and an ideal aristocracy, often in distant space and time.

In addition to romantic aristocrats, three other classes that existed in England at the time are portrayed in Gilbert's comedies: the upper-bourgeois civil servant (Sir Joseph in *Pinafore,* General Stanley in *Pirates of Penzance,* the peers in *Iolanthe,* the judges in *Trial by Jury*); below them, the functionary officers (colonels, majors and lieutenants in *Patience* and *Yeoman of the Guard,* the captain in *Pinafore*) who are more blindly adherent to the military ideal than capitalistically ambitious; lowest of all, the realistic plebeian of the industrial society, a hard-bitten and selfish underling like Dick Deadeye in *Pinafore.* He is juxtaposed against the pastoral Ralph Rackstraw as romantically wrong/actually right about the nonprobability of a tar's marrying the daughter of his captain. The mock plot proves/disproves the rightness of the romantic attitude. Ralph and Josephine have been attracted to each other, he by her aristocratic beauty, she by his pastoral simplicity; it turns out that he is actually an aristocrat to the manner born, and rightful captain of the ship. As in *A Winter's Tale,* it is suggested that only the born aristocrat can perfect the pastoral ideal, itself only a version of aristocratic life. All normal plebeians are cringing Dick Deadeyes and unscrupulous Autolycuses. While the tragic

Melville could conceive of the natural aristocrat Billy Budd becoming nonprobable hanged god in the brutal probability of eighteenth-century British naval life, the pastoral ideal to the realistic, probable eye of comedy is a romantic fake.

One other class, the nonprobable pariah, is singled out for more jocund treatment than usual in comedy: pirates in *The Pirates of Penzance,* fairies in *Iolanthe,* the sorcerer and his female equivalents like the wandering Buttercup in *Pinafore,* the poets in *Patience.* Still, as in Aristophanes, they are expelled by revelation of the selfish half of their motivation.

In the probabilities of the classes, there are the probabilities of generation: youth, middle age, old age. Youth is idealistic, fanciful, and unable to cope with the problems of life through lack of experience. Middle age is worldly wise and coldly practical, old age, doddering and indulgent, or morose like King Gama in *Princess Ida.* In marriage, income, and position, these classes and age groups must remain in the grooves of probability to achieve happiness. Occasionally a selfish member of one group will try to trade off his advantages to the favor of his disadvantages with the member of another class and age group. But pluses and minuses which cancel in logical mathematics do not do so in the pure action of life. The upper-class, middle-aged Sir Joseph in *Pinafore* thinks he will balance equally by marrying the middle-class, young Josephine. He argues that class is no barrier to marriage—and she interprets his remarks in favor of herself and Ralph. Conservative comedy laughs at the nonprobability of all attempts to cross class lines.

APPEARANCE AND REALITY

In a highly mannered society the natural man, selfish, intuitional, and individualistic, is concealed behind the social mask of impartiality, reason, and social duty. Comedy in the nonprobability of its saturnalian excess and its stage (not life) existence, presents the natural man in paradox with the mask he wears in society. Falstaff and Trinculo, who indulge their appetites to the full, pay for neglecting the social mask by being ritually expelled from the society.

119

In Gilbert's comedies the appearance of all altruistic ideas masks the reality of selfish desire. Sir Joseph actually does not advocate mixing the classes by marriage; he merely wants an excuse to get his hands on the luscious Josephine. In *The Gondoliers,* Marco and Giuseppe renounce monarchy in theory while members of the lower classes:

> As we abhor oppression, we abhor kings: as we detest vain-glory, we detest rank: as we despise effeminacy, we despise wealth. We are Venetian gondoliers—your equals in everything except our calling, and in that at once your masters and your servants.

But when Don Alhambra del Bolero, the Grand Inquisitioner, tells them that perhaps they are kings themselves, they change their ideas very fast:

> Well, as to that, of course there are kings and kings. When I say that I detest kings, I mean I detest *bad* kings . . . Now I can conceive a kind of king—an ideal king—the creature of my fancy, you know—who would be absolutely unobjectionable. A king, for instance, who would abolish taxes and make everything cheap, except gondolas. . . .

The mock medievalism of Bunthorne in *Patience* emerges as a mask for his selfish bid for attention. Elaborate in their juxtaposition of extreme selfishness with extreme manners are the subtle discussions of the three peers in *Iolanthe,* each of whom is determined to get the hand of Phyllis while remaining in masked amity with his rivals. The general in *The Pirates of Penzance* is quite capable of telling a lie to save his skin; and his lie, shamefaced as it is, implies that in the pure action of military life truth–falsehood is not an operative distinction. Nevertheless, the code of honor as mask of the mannered warrior demands rigid adherence to truth in lip-service and appearance. The Spartan boy is a thief only when caught stealing and in the American Army the officer's gonorrhea is very often put down on medical reports as nonspecific urethritis. Comedy in its awareness of the probable knows that the mask of the soldier—as a jolly, religious, handsome, moral, upright, intelligent Briton—conceals a brutal selfishness that realistically contradicts all those qualities. Yet in an empire the more gullible and weaker citizens who benefit from the system protect themselves against the harsher realities of some parts necessary to the system's structure by weaving a romantic fancy. The bourgeois imagines to himself a type of soldier who never existed. Gilbert and Sullivan imply the reality by jibing at the romantic appearance:

> *A British tar is a soaring soul,*
> *As free as a mountain bird,*
> *His energetic fist should be ready to resist*
> *A dictatorial word . . .*
> *His eyes should flash with an inborn fire,*
> *His brow with scorn be wrung;*
> *He never should bow down to a domineering frown,*
> *Or the tang of a tyrant tongue.*
> *His foot should stamp and his throat should growl,*
> *His hair should twirl and his face should scowl.*

But we all know that a soldier must take orders and that military life is more brutalizing than liberating to the soul. The probability of military life, as Shaw's *Arms and the Man* also shows, is quite different from what the romantic bourgeois imagines. The average citizen shies away from the brute realities of military cost to maintain an empire abroad and keep police discipline at home. While Mabel, General Stanley's romantic daughter in *The Pirates of Penzance* shouts to the police:

> *Go, ye heroes, go to glory.*
> *Though you die in combat gory*
> *Ye shall live in song and story.*
> *Go to immortality!*
> *Go to death, and go to slaughter;*
> *Die, and every Cornish daughter*
> *With her tears your grave shall water.*
> *Go, ye heroes, go and die!*

the police themselves, who "uncomfortable feel, when the foeman bares his steel," are not so enthusiastic about becoming a sacrifice to maintain order:

121

> *Though to us it's evident*
> > *Tarantara! tarantara!*
> *These intentions are well meant*
> > *Tarantara!*
> *Such expressions don't appear*
> > *Tarantara! tarantara!*
> *Calculated men to cheer*
> > *Tarantara!*

But police will admit this only on the nonprobable comic stage. In normal life they blindly subscribe to the code of honor. In his transcendence of romantic motives, and his ordering of them under selfish categories, the comic poet predicts and endorses the society. His laughter at the roughnesses—the captain's cat o' nine tails in *Pinafore,* the Inquisitioner's torture chambers in *The Gondoliers*—accepts them as a hard but necessary instrument for the joyous success of bourgeois existence. The mask is first taken off, and then shown as a social necessity for protection against the unmasked basic selfishness of man. Things may be at odds for a while in this normal system, and under the nonprobable moonlight (daylight and moonlight are often used in Gilbert as probable–wonderful symbols), a not-too-bright captain may worry about the discrepancies:

> *Fair moon, to thee I sing,*
> *Bright regent of the heavens,*
> *Say, why is everything*
> *Either at sixes or at sevens?*
> *I have lived hitherto*
> *Free from breath of slander*
> *Beloved by all my crew—*
> *A really popular commander.*
> *But now my kindly crew rebel,*
> *My daughter to a tar is partial,*
> *Sir Joseph storms, and, sad to tell,*
> *He threatens a court martial!*
> *Fair moon, to thee I sing,*
> *Bright regent of the heavens,*
> *Say, why is everything*
> *Either at sixes or at sevens?*

122

The poor captain has followed all the norms of experience in running his ship, and cannot understand why they do not solve all problems. But in the end balance is restored, the normal social life of classes and ages is resumed under the necessary though false masks of conventional duty and appearance.

The plots of Gilbert's comedies seem not to occur at all. Each seems a figment, an illusion, a mockery of the stage itself. As the plays proceed in their delicate parodies of Wagner, Italian opera, and Latin comedy, we are subtly made to feel that it is all not taking place, that the actors and we ourselves are cavalierly inventing the plot. Most comedy at points will violate/thereby affirm the third-personal stage convention; the Gilbert and Sullivan operas in undertone violate that convention by the whole play itself. At critical moments in *Ruddigore* and *The Pirates of Penzance,* for example, an appeal is made to the Union Jack and to Queen Victoria, with the assumption that the villain cannot flout those sacred fetiches and must therefore be stalemated by the soldiers of the right. The crux of these plays is so absurd that it implies they could not happen at all, nor their surrounding action be probable. Many of these plays occur in non-probable space and time, in countries which seem invented for the play only and are implied to be so in the play itself. Japan, Utopia, Olympus, medieval Venice, feudal England—we cannot believe in them as we can in Shakespeare's Bohemia or even Aristophanes' *Cloudcuckooland,* because the playwright himself implies in undertone that they do not exist. The motifs of family curse (*Ruddigore*), discovery of the changeling child (*Iolanthe, Pinafore, The Gondoliers*) and wedding of the romantic couple who conquer the opposition of the middle-aged for the lifelong courtship of marriage—all this is mocked covertly as mere appearance, the stuff of romance. These plots are not ordinary comic plots. Contrast *Princess Ida* with its source, *Love's Labour's Lost,* or *The Sorcerer* with *A Midsummer Night's Dream.* The patterns of marriage, success, expulsion of abnormality, generation, all basic patterns in comedy, are there; but the ritual events do not really take place. The playwright hints that, after all, they are merely invented for the stage. Not only in specific paradoxes about bourgeois belief/realistic actuality is appearance/reality represented, but also in the ambiguity of tone in the play itself.

This is very evident in *Iolanthe* where the fairies who belong to no generation and the half-man half-sprite Strephon, son of the affair between fairy Iolanthe and a peer, convert the probable peers at the end of the play to their way of life. Instead of wonderful individuals being expelled, the highest diplomats assume abnormality. Peers become Peris (a Persian fairy), and admission to the aristocracy of their house will be open to merit alone by a competitive intellectual examination. In other plays, however, the pariahs must be revealed as true aristocrats in disguise before the society will embrace them. The pirates in *The Pirates of Penzance* are a "shy lot," burning with search for the wonderful in their pariahism and bored with the probability of their job, precisely like the highway robbers in *Man and Superman*. When General Stanley and the police finally bring them around by an appeal to Queen Victoria after all else has failed, the pirates turn out to be peers in disguise. The nonprobable outsiders adjust to the nonprobable aristocracy; actuality/disguise becomes disguise/actuality, and General Stanley's daughters, who shuddered at them when they were pirates, are quite willing to marry the "poor wandering ones" now that they are peers. The general, in illogical selfishness, quotes a proverb about the middle-aged pirates ("peers will be peers, and youth will have its fling") and the play ends, as most of Gilbert's do, with the prospect of a marriage. Similar is the transformation of Nanki-Poo in the *Mikado*, a prince disguised as nonprobable wandering minstrel. The society will execute this pariah as sacrifice, presumably for kissing Yum-Yum. This Japanese/Victorian maiden, attracted as she is to Nanki-Poo, is reluctant to marry him when she must follow her husband in a month to death. When he is revealed a prince, she is once more glad to become his wife.

The ladies of *Princess Ida,* who have symbolically fortified themselves in the spiritual speculation/virginity of Castle Adamant, are overcome, like the men in *Love's Labour's Lost,* by their own natural bodily appetites; they abandon wonderful speculation for probable marriage.[2]

---

[2]The spirit-body duality in this play is reflected in the names of the characters: Greek (spirit): Hilarion, Gama, Ida, Cyril, Florian, Psyche, Melissa, Chloe, Ada; versus Barbarian (body): Arac, Guron, Hildebrand. The name "Scynthius" combines both elements: Scythia, the hyperborean barbarian land of antiquity, and Cynthia, goddess of the moon.

Not so happy is the lot of other abnormal characters. John Wellington Wells in *The Sorcerer* is burned at a rollicking crowd's desire in the fires of hell; and poor Bunthorne in *Patience* is worsted both by the officers who have been courting the maidens and the bourgeois clerk Grosvenor. In the end he is left without a bride.

In the *Bab Ballads* especially, Gilbert had more directly attacked another nonprobable member of society, the clergyman. For this he was denounced by a comedian of quite another stamp, Charles Lutwidge Dodgson, who wrote in *The Theatre Magazine* in 1888:

> Mr. Gilbert seems to have a craze for making bishops and clergy-men contemptible . . . That clever song "The Pale Young Curate," with its charming music, is to me simply painful. I seem to see him as he goes home at night, pale and worn with the day's work, perhaps sick with the pestilent atmosphere of a noisome garret where, at the risk of his life, he has been comforting a dying man . . . And is your sense of humour, my reader, so keen that you can laugh at that man? Then at least be consistent. Laugh also at that pale young doctor, whom you have summoned in such hot haste to your own dying child; ay, and laugh also at that pale young soldier, as he sinks on the trampled battlefield, and reddens the dust with his life-blood for the honour of Old England!

THE FANCIES OF THE MATHEMATICAL CLERGYMAN

As the barrister Gilbert wrote comedies on the pure action of law and social life, so Charles Dodgson the Oxford mathematics don composed fantasies of logical speculation. In his work are merged the two forms of the probable, comedy and logic. Though he relegated them into separate compartments of his life, the essential relation of comedy to logic merges in the totality of the personality, just as the two types of work permeate one another in his writing. For the speculative logic of the mathematical treatises and puzzles is often comically playful, and all the artistic fantasies of his poems and tales are full of mock logic. In his serious abstract writing, Dodgson discussed many of the probable topics that later concerned George Bernard Shaw: vivisection, the problem of slaughtering

125

animals for food (the child wakes up to this in *Alice, Through the Looking-Glass, Sylvie and Bruno*), the poverty of the working classes, logical problems on God and the Church. He spent his spare time taking photographs, writing comic poems, and constructing playful mathematical puzzles. Other probable topics occupied his attention, from the best method of running a tennis tournament to the problem of academic salaries. Whether discussing the nature of sin and God's justice or the method of taking votes at particular kinds of meetings, Dodgson's writing follows the rigid pattern of logical propositions and conclusions. Usually he is relativistic enough merely to state alternative propositions and formally to make no claim of choice among them.

Rose Maybud, the pastoral maiden in *Ruddigore,* is always consulting her etiquette book (the probability of manners), showing at once the laughable restrictions of Victorian society and the nonprobability of trying to perform manners from books rather than in action itself. Similarly, Carroll in a comic paper (*Hints for Etiquette*) and throughout *Alice in Wonderland* and *Through the Looking-Glass* is always presenting manners as absurd and confusing to the child; easily offended caterpillars, overbearing duchesses, and mad tea parties.

THE WONDER OF CHILDHOOD, THE PROBABILITY OF ADULTHOOD

Dodgson was crippled into permanent childhood by the hold his family exercised on him spiritually. How domineering his father must have been can be judged by the fact that only two of his eleven children later married; and Charles, it may be fairly said, entered orders not from religious fervor, but because he was too retiring to face the problem of marriage. That his Oxford position at the time made celibacy the norm is only another facet of his retreat. At times in his serious work he was capable of hardy insights into pure-action probabilities:

> I invited an aged beggar in to "sit by my fire, and talk the night away" [It was immediately after reading Goldsmith's "Deserted Village"]. True it is that he told me nothing interesting, and that he took the hall-clock with him when he departed in the morning.

126

And in his paper on vivisection he puts this statement into the mouth of the scientist:

> The lust for scientific knowledge is our real guiding principle. The lessening of human suffering is a mere dummy set up to amuse sentimental dreamers.

But most of the time the problems of his age—classes, labor, the Empire, unnecessary repression of sexual desire—are seen only jocularly through the dream eyes of the child.

Alice in Wonderland was begun as an inspiration while rowing on secluded waters with three little girls. As often in spontaneous writings of the sexually repressed, sexual symbolism is rife at the beginning of the work. Alice jumps down a dark hole after a rabbit, floats in a well, crawls in the dark to get into a lush garden. She grows small from drinking, then big with an elongated neck from eating. She grows small again by putting her hand in the rabbit's glove, and bathes in the tears she shed while big. Empson in the *Alice* chapter of *Some Versions of Pastoral* traces many other evidences of sexual symbolism in that work, among them the birth trauma in Alice's growing monstrously big and curling up in the rabbit's house.

Dodgson retreated into life at Oxford, playing games with little girls and himself all his life, his serious duties besides a light teaching load being such trivia as managing a Senior Common Room. Though he was ordained, he looked with horror on running a parish and to escape it purposely took no orders higher than deacon. Yet he found it necessary to split even this secluded life into waking mathematics professor and dreaming comic writer. This split existed not in name only; Dodgson was always highly embarrassed, often angry, when people referred to his fantasies, even after they had become popular for years all over England. His personal relationships seem to have been only childish; his business life at Oxford reminds one of little boys solemnly playing games with management. He seems never to have had a deep friendship with any of his colleagues. Most of his social hours were spent with his spiritual equals, little children, particularly pretty little girls. There is no denying the morbid side of this attachment, with its raining kisses and little jealousies. He often had the little girls pose for him in the nude, and would brook no jocularity; once Isa Bowman drew a caricature of him, whereupon he went flaming red and tore it up in anger. He always chose only pretty girls, many of them actresses, for his favorites, and always expressed worries over society's attitude to this, a sign of guilt feeling. Yet one would not go so far as Mrs. Liddell, the mother of Alice, who violently distrusted the motives of Dodgson's attachment to her daughter. He may possibly have had in the back of his mind a later marriage with her, but the actual relationship was that of one child to another. Dodgson in his own mind was either the dirty little boy (the pigboy in *Alice,* Tweedledum and Tweedledee in *Through the Looking-Glass,* Uggug in *Sylvie and Bruno*) or the shy, retiring White Knight, the pale, ridiculous courtier of the little maiden.

In his comic writings he viewed a probable adult world through the wonder of a child's eyes. Once Alice (Dodgson-phallus) is initiated by being born, growing big (also sexually), she meets all sorts of strange people and strange manners. She finds that the mouse, whom she symbolically meets while swimming in the tears she shed while big, hates the cat because cats eat mice; she had never thought this through, and it is a disturbing revelation to her. She then sees the queerness of probable politics in a Caucus Race. A caterpillar gives advice about manners, but she is very confused. "I wish the creatures wouldn't be so easily offended!" she says. The directions he gives her seem ambiguous and she doesn't know what to do. Besides meeting obvious sexual symbols (fish, the frog with powdered hair), she is brought into the mannered action of courts and tea parties. The Duchess with her baby, the Cheshire Cat, the March Hare, Dormouse, and Mad Hatter at their party, the King and Queen of Hearts, the mock turtle and the gryphon—all are queerly individualistic adults who seem gruff and unknowable to the child let loose in their hostile world of mannered pure action.

Empson sees Alice as a pastoral hero, "The Child as Swain"; but she almost always fails in this strange land, and her success is only in returning home to childhood. The proud, the dozing dinner guest, the man with an obsession, the perpetually lugubrious, are at once burlesqued and shown as puzzling to the poor child who encounters them. This world attacks her symbolically. It says "off with her head" at every turn, and perpetually embarrasses her. Finally it puts her to trial; but at that moment she can escape from the wonder of nonprobable dream, which to the child/retreating Dodgson is the probability of actual adult life. Alice-Dodgson can be rewaked by the child sister into the happy child life of nice food and walks in the summer garden.

But Peter Pan's companions all grow up into probable lawyers and judges; he alone is left to the wonder of piracy and romance with little girls. So while Dodgson lived out of generation in the fairyland of retreat with children, his little friends would grow from that kind summer into the rough winter of adulthood. Summer-winter symbolism for child-hood-adulthood is frequent in Carroll, as in the dedication of *Through the Looking-Glass*:

> *No thought of me shall find a place*
> *In thy young life's hereafter—*
> *Enough that now thou wilt not fail*
> *To listen to my fairy tale.*
>
> *A tale begun in other days,*
> *When summer suns were glowing—*
> *A simple chime, that served to time*
> *The rhythm of our rowing—*
> *Whose echoes live in memory yet*
> *Though envious years would say "forget."*
>
> *Come, hearken then, ere voice of dread,*
> *With bitter tidings laden*
> *Shall summon to unwelcome bed*
> *A melancholy maiden!*
> *We are but older children, dear,*
> *Who fret to find our bedtime near.*

129

> *Without, the frost, the blinding snow,*
> *The storm-wind's moody madness—*
> *Within, the firelight's ruddy glow,*
> *And childhood's nest of gladness.*
> *The magic words shall hold thee fast;*
> *Thou shalt not heed the raving blast.*

Double meanings can be read here, not only as Empson suggests, in the maiden's bed, but throughout the whole poem. Carroll seems to mean the bed primarily as death, but it is also, as always in comedy, the bed of sex, the death of childhood for the adult. Not only Alice, but Dodgson himself "frets to find his bedtime near."

Alice in Wonderland, the child's journey into the queerness of adult manners and personalities, came to Dodgson in 1862 when he was thirty and still adjusting himself to life at Oxford. It was written within the year after he was ordained a deacon. Nine years later, when he had settled into that life, he explored in *Through the Looking Glass* the relativism of life/dream, logic/illogic, subject/object. Alice moves along a chessboard in the inside-out realm behind the looking glass, where the logical paradoxes of life are reduced to nonsensical patterns by reversing them. Even the table of contents to the book is in the form of a chess diagram and problem. The Looking-Glass creatures are real/unreal; talking flowers, the Jabberwock, living chessmen, Humpty Dumpty (stuffy middle-aged man/petulant bad boy), and the Walrus and the Carpenter populate this mannered land of illogic and explain it to the uncomfortable/searching Alice. To Dodgson, who often got inspiration in dreams for parts of his books, the distinction between the lives of waking and dreaming was more than normally illusory. His ghost in *Phantasmagoria* is quite probable and possesses a code of manners:

> *"Perhaps," he said, "You first transgressed*
> *The laws of hospitality:*
> *All ghosts instinctively detest*
> *The man that fails to treat his guest*
> *With proper cordiality."*

130

The elaborate relativity of this piece has enticed many later serious thinkers on the probable to quote from *Through the Looking-Glass*—Korszybsky, Russell, and Whitehead among others.

In this mock kingdom, with its two opposing factions of Red (blood, action) and White (soul, nerves) occurs the battle between the probable Lion and the wonderful Unicorn who thinks that Alice, a little child, is a fabulous monster. The White Knight (Dodgson) with his little invention that holds clothes and sandwiches befriends Alice, sings her a song about haddocks' eyes (all the songs in this book are about fish, a phallic symbol). He leads her as a chess pawn to the eighth square, where she becomes queen and finds on her head a golden crown. The Red Queen and White Queen, however, are loath to accept her; they give her an elaborate and embarrassing examination before they finally acknowledge her. At her dinner party, she still has all sorts of trouble with manners. "I should never have known who were the right people to invite," she says. As the two queens squeeze her, she finds herself once more in the room of her home squeezing the Red Queen, who turns out to be her little kitten. The book ends with Alice's logical remark, "Now, Kitty, let's consider who it was that dreamed it all." Elaborate and dainty as *Through the Looking-Glass* is, it suffers from too great a self-consciousness on Carroll's part; his care to insert the meanings into these imaginative works made them progressively more dull; his first book, *Alice in Wonderland,* is his best.

Sylvie and Bruno (1889), much later tales of voyages to Elfeston, chiefly discuss political topics: the meaning of money, socialism, the rights of the lower classes, taxation, mock plots to overthrow a government. They also contain in much duller form the stock motifs of Carroll: tedious mock logic, the explanations of an absurdly logical professor and "I" (Dodgson) to the little boy and girl, the fish poems, the reversal of time, hunting snails, the shock of eating animals, and so on. But the fancy of the young mathematics professor became the dull wit of the consciously moralizing don; the tendency toward contrived fable rather than artful nonsense, already present in *Through the Looking-Glass,* has conquered. Carroll's work gets more mawkish as he stagnates into the retreat of his unnatural existence; his last volume, a posthumous book of poems, *Three Sunsets,* is almost trash. Instead of growing, the don worked the same mathematical puzzles, pursued and entertained the same little girls, labored in his logic the same topics, and dodged insomnia and the Snark (snake-shark, both sexual symbols) till his death. The wonder of creating comedy was shut off into a nonprobable compartment of his life; and what might have been artistic growth became moralistic obsession. In a trip to Russia he seems to have visited only the Greek Orthodox cathedrals. The keenness of his playful relativistic insights into logic and mathematics never penetrated his serious writings. An awareness of the problems of his time was shunted off into the playful mockery of fable for little girls. He exhausted the possibilities of his subject for himself in two books and a few poems; all the rest was idle repetition.

The basic elements of comedy are present in his work: manners, logic, social topics, beast-fable, the dull reasoner, the ungovernable rogue of natural appetite. But in the pattern of his life the creation of this comedy took the form of escape, the conscious nonprobability of fancy. It is this which has made the surrealists, romanticists of the nonprobable, adopt Carroll as a prototype of their own work. And it is this which limits the scope of both his life and his art.

SAMUEL BUTLER · THE RATIONALISM OF SATIRE

The satirist, a logical rationalist, views the world through the lens of probability. He sees that it rewards such merit as his with obscurity and neglect. Not ethical uprightness gains rewards on earth, but the conniving and slavish pure-action techniques of politicians. Even if he is a clergyman like Swift or in high favor with the emperor like Petronius, he cannot abide the neglect of goodness and the flourishing of evil in the world. Seeing the probable and his own nonprobability, his reason tells him that he is cheated. In passive hybris he refuses to take the wonder of humility, and prefers to mete as justice to the world his individual scorn, the tiny spurt of his own venom. All writers on the probable touch at least occasionally on satire. In probable novels there is almost always a running undertone of satire on manners (for example, the bourgeois courtships in *Buddenbrooks*). In the savage laughter of Aristophanes and Rabelais or the mild joshing of Gilbert, the comic writer takes strongly or weakly his revenge for his own expulsion on the norms of the society he is preserving.

Satirists themselves differ in tone, like comedians. The savage bitterness of Juvenal and Swift, the sardonic hopelessness of Petronius, are as foreign as tragedy itself from the sober and straightforward rationalism of Samuel Butler. Like Molière, he is in dead earnest. He believes that logic will progress in the world, where a wiser satirist like Swift knows that folly and illogic are eternal. Though Butler admired Swift, his work always strains toward the serious allegory of Bunyan, especially in *Erewhon*. Allegory, being rationalist, is always probable and nearly always satirical. Even in literature Butler had little taste for the wonderful; common sense was his guide, as he professes in his notebooks:

> I have never read, and never, I am afraid, shall read a line of Keats or Shelley or Coleridge or Wordsworth . . . The poets of the day are names to me and nothing more . . . there is no concealing the fact that it is the business, practical side of literature and not the poetical and imaginative—I mean literature applied to the solving of some difficult problem which may be usefully solved—that alone fires me with hot desire to devour and imitate it. That, and the battering down of falsehood to the utmost of my poor ability.

In the smug probability of this Mill-like utilitarianism, he thought that the essence of Christianity was common sense, and regarded himself a true Christian. He mocked revelation; in the "Rights of Animals" chapter of *Erewhon* he speaks of an old prophet "more or less fussy" who had ample leisure to speculate only because the state supported him (yet Butler had a private income!). This prophet carried even logic to excess and "wanted . . . to put all sorts of matters on a logical basis, which people whose time is money are content to accept on no basis at all." The shift between reason and pure action, the poles of probable thought, is in all of Butler's work:

133

As a matter of course, the basis on which he decided that duty alone could rest was one that afforded no standing-room for many of the old-established habits of the people. These, he assured them, were all wrong, and whenever any one ventured to differ from him, he referred the matter to the unseen power with which he alone was in direct communication, and the unseen power invariably assured him that he was right.

Erewhon, Butler's first book of wide scope and popularity, was based partly on his own five years' experience as a sheep farmer in New Zealand. "I" in the country over the range, Erewhon, was driven into this strange land, like Gulliver, by an unknown fortune and on an uncertain route. While Swift uses physical size and position (the floating island Britain over the subject Ireland), Butler uses physical and commercial analogies for England. The new/probable country is both satire on England and a covert representation of his own ideals. He expounds his views on crime as product of environment by making disease a crime in *Erewhon* and showing the corruption and stupidity of the attendant laws. The English analogues are conspicuously implied. The colleges of Unreason, unlike those in Swift's Laputa, closely resemble Oxford and Cambridge; there young men study hypotheticals and learn to compose in hypothetical language (Latin and Greek), but are left in utter ignorance of probable pure action and commerce. Machines have been abolished in Erewhon, on the fallacious ground that their development in natural selection would lead them to supplant men. Butler here repeats his attack on Darwinism; he himself believed that cunning, not the development of limbs and organs, was the basic process in natural selection, and that Darwin's belief could be reasoned out to the conclusion of the Erewhonians. Here again his rationalism is paramount.

People in Erewhon pay the greatest respect to the Musical Banks (Church of England) but actually do little more than lip-service to them. The traveller is surprised to see so few people at the bank he visits, and he ridicules in his account the faith/neglect of the country in them:

> When they [the cashiers/priests] were in the room every one would talk as though all currency save that of the Musical Banks should be

abolished; and yet they knew perfectly well that even the cashiers themselves hardly used the Musical Bank money more than other people. It was expected of them that they should appear to do so, but this was all.

Later, as the inhabitants of Gilbert's *Utopia* worship England, so in *Erewhon Revisited* the darkhaired swarthy people has made a god in the cult of Sunchildism out of the blond Butler. The real goddess of these people/England was Ydgrun (Mrs. Grundy) whom they seldom mentioned. She was the goddess of respectability who demanded that one run his life so as not to offend his neighbor. Those who were cleverest at following her dictates she rewarded with material prosperity.

The paradox between comedy's rationalism and its expulsion of the nonprobable rationalist occurs in the life of the satirist, the pattern of which is often different from his writings. Swift had much of the passive hybris in Molière: like the miser, he was penurious; like the misanthrope he was plagued with a hatred of the species; like the old courtier in *L'Ecole des Femmes,* he raised Esther Johnson from girlhood according to his own ideas and was always attracted to younger women. His adventures in the realm of probability always met with disaster, because of his bluntness and anxiety. Though he was a clergyman, he persisted in seeing all from the probable point of view. Butler, raised like Dodgson in the starved atmosphere of a nineteenth-century clerical family, revolted from his home life and attacked his parents in the posthumous *Way of All Flesh*. Yet he never questioned the economic structure of his own society, which benefited him greatly. Like Herbert Spencer, he approved of the jungle laws of free enterprise, considering them a type of natural selection. Spencer disbelieved in charity and Butler thought that any rich man was entitled to his goods, obtained through work or inheritance, because they represent what society strives for. He practiced a rebellious individualism, yet saw society as a machine; like many nineteenth-century sociologists, he even made elaborate mechanical parallels between the machine and the life of a city. He did not see the contradiction between logic and the logically-selected norms of pure action (which equals the satirist/society paradox in different focus). "I" in *Erewhon* wants to impress us as an

135

honest and logical person; yet with little provocation he lies to the ship captain who rescued him and Arowhena from the sea. Butler rebukes the prophet for living off society, but he himself spent most of his own time in economically wasteful speculations: elaborate investigations of the topography and authorship of the *Odyssey,* a reordering of Shakespeare's sonnets. Though espousing social utilitarianism, he spent a large share of his time studying and producing art, not only his writings, but painting and music. On the former he spent years as a student with little fruit. Neglected by the society he reasoned about, he frittered his energies in the dilettantism of professional rebel and mediocre artist.

There is something unsatisfactory about nineteenth-century writers on the probable. Like Flaubert, Butler idealized the life of the nonintellectual, the peasant of Italy. And like most writers in his age, he was unable to tap the roots of human feeling by becoming a man among men. He stood apart from the race in speculation and refrained from partaking of its deepest joys and sorrows. With his enlightened views on sex, he still did not marry. But neither did Swift; and he is far deeper and more human than the disappointed barrister, the Oxford teacher of geometry, the self-righteous dilettante.

CERVANTES · FIELDING · FINNEGANS WAKE

Then, stealing his thunder, but in the befitting legomena of the smaller country, (probable words, possibly said, of field family gleaming) a bit duskish and flavoured with a smile, seein as ow his thoughts consisted chiefly of the cheerio, he aptly sketched for our soontobe second parents (sukand see whybe!) the touching seene. The solence of that stilling! Here one might a fin fell. Boomster rombombonant! It scenes like a landescape from Wildu Picturescu or some seem on some dimb Arras, dumb as Mum's mutyness, this mimage of the seventy-seventh kusin of kristansen is odable to os across the wineless Ere no oedor nor mere eerie nor liss potent of suggestion than in the tales of the tingmount. (Prigged!)

—FINNEGANS WAKE

The careers of Cervantes and Dostoievsky are strikingly similar; throughout the sufferings and wanderings of their early lives, both show clearly the desire to create. Both had early military training and both spent long periods in the army—Cervantes as an enlisted soldier, Dostoievsky in forced service after the commutation of his Siberian sentence. Dostoievsky spent five years in Siberia, thinking that the sentence would last his lifetime; Cervantes was five years the slave of a renegade in Algiers, with the threat continually over his head of flogging, torture, and death. Both were sentenced to death; Dostoievsky for political radicalism, Cervantes for attempting to escape from his Algerian master. Yet the brooding Dostoievsky could always relate his punishment to his own guilt, whereas for the brave Cervantes it was a blind fate which caused his suffering. While Dostoievsky created wonderful tragic novels of the soul's journey, Cervantes wrote of the pain incurred at the hands of the probable by a comic idealist.

A military organization is the most probable of human governmental structures. It has a clearly defined purpose and a hierarchy of codes and regulations arranged for the achievement of that purpose. Though in its official machinery it logically provides for the wonderful with the function of the chaplain, the soul of the individual otherwise counts for nothing. Man is a probable machine, the doer of a unit of work, an obedient beast. Transgression of this basic law by disagreement (insubordination) or withdrawal (desertion) is the deepest crime, because it strikes at the heart of the system. Individual judgment on values and standards can take force away from an objective; and the military organization by its nature considers only its single objective. The soldier learns to distrust all individual ideals, all dreams, all searchings of the soul, as moonshine; for he sees with convincing clarity how these ideals can cause his social group greater pain.

In his long service as an enlisted soldier, in battle, in the arduous five years of slavery, Cervantes was brought to an overwhelming awareness of individual folly and social probability. He must have come to distrust the two literary traditions in the Spain of his youth—the romantic pastoral of the natural aristocrat/refined shepherd, and the romantic tale of knightly adventure and courtly love. If he had ever been attracted to these two traditions by their ideal sensitivity, they must have come to seem wonderful delusions in the course of his hard probable experience—all the more so because the bourgeois men and women of his time were enticed by them. Don Quixote in that novel is not the only one who reads—or writes!—romances. In the comic motifs of parody on romantic books and mock voyage into the wonderful, Cervantes created Don Quixote, the ridiculous searcher, the self-deluded individualist, the meddling hero who perpetually misinterprets the probable world and is automatically served with pain for his violation of probability.

Don Quixote was a well-to-do farmer in Mancha, prosperously living a probable life, until he became fascinated with Amadis de Gaule, *Orlando Furioso,* the tales of the Round Table, and other knightly adventure stories. Symbolically, he sold "many acres of arable land" to buy these books, and finally became so enamoured of them that he resolved to become a knight. Embarking on long adventures, he incurs shock after shock because he insists on interpreting in idealistic terms the realistic events which happen to him. A probable inn is a wonderful castle; its keeper who demands rent, a courtly lord who entertains the Don; and two whores, chaste ladies of the castle. The knight, as a wonderful individual not identified with other human beings but helping them like a god, is exempt from social, probable duties:

> Come hither, O you that be no troopers, but thieves in troop, and robbers of highways by permission of the Holy Brotherhood; come hither, I say, and tell me, who was that jolter-head that did subscribe or ratify a warrant for the attaching of a knight as I am? Who was he that knows not how knights-errant are exempted from all tribunals? And how that their sword is the law, their valour the bench, and their wills the statutes of their courts? . . . What knight-errant did ever pay tribute, subsidy, taillage, carriage, or passage over water?

Dubbed a knight by the whores, Don Quixote sallies forth into the world, but is so beaten, bled, and maimed at the hands of those with whom he "jousts" that he perforce must return home. His household retinue burn the books which have turned their master from a manager into a searcher, telling him that the library was destroyed by enchantment.

But his passion grows again. He induces one of his tenant farmers, Sancho Panza, to be his squire by promising him the governorship of an island when the Don becomes emperor. Looking back on the "happy times and fortunate ages" of the bygone Golden Age, as Peisthetairos does in the *Birds,* and taking as his patron saints the Cid, the Knights of the Round Table, and others, he goes on the dusty road in search of the wonderful once more. He makes a show of knowing and embracing the hardships of the road:

> The profession of my exercise doth not license or permit me to do other. Good days, cockering and ease were invented for soft courtiers, but travel, unrest and arms were only invented and made for those which the world terms knights-errant, of which number I myself (although unworthy) am one, and the least of them all.

In the crux of actual practice, his asceticism always yields to the selfish desire for good food and a soft bed; poor Sancho Panza scarcely understands the difference between his master's professions and actions. Don Quixote expounds constantly his faithful love for Dulcinea, but when Maritornes enters his dark room in the inn to sleep with someone else, he catches her by the wrist, imagines (so Cervantes says in irony) all her faults to be virtues—her stinking breath, perfume, for example— and holds her fast till he is thwacked by the other man. Tilting windmills is justly taken as a symbol for all his activity: seeing the probable machine as a wonderful giant, he ventures confidently with his lance against the cosmos, and is twirled in the air automatically by the probable (which he interprets as wonderful). Always he is beaten up, bathed in his own blood. His bones are broken, or he is hung by the hand, or stoned by the criminals he unwisely freed from chains. The romances of other knights in the face of Don Quixote's experience are ironically implied to be false:

> " . . . And truly (says Sancho Panza) you have one of the evil-fa-vouredest countenances of late that ever I saw; which proceedeth

either of your being tired after this battle or else through the loss of your teeth." "This is not the reason," said Don Quixote, "but rather it hath seemed fit to the wise man, to whose charge is left the writing of my history, that I take some appellative name, as all other knights of yore have done; for one called himself the Knight of the Burning Sword [compare the *Knight of the Burning Pestle,* Beaumont and Fletcher's similar parody], another that of the Unicorn; this, him of the Phoenix; the other, that of the Damsels; another, the Knight of the Griffin. . . . some other the Knight of Death [note the wonderful titles]; . . . call me the Knight of the Ill-Favored Face, as I mean to call myself from henceforth."

The more frequently he errs and the more knocks he receives, the more confidently and unflinchingly the Don attacks a probable cosmos which again and again knocks him down in sure defeat. His failing past is transformed into success by an imaginative memory. Shut in a cage as a madman at the end of Part I, he obliviously rants on in perfect calm about the ideals and deeds of his knightly search. Every man's hand is against the Don's, and at one point even Sancho Panza betrays him. Yet he conceives of himself as a wonderful hero who is performing good deeds for the world.

When Don Quixote individually starts out to perform glorious deeds for himself and society, he wounds the society as well as himself. The galllantry of the individual is a selfishness costly to himself and to others. He "rescues" a young boy who is being whipped by his master for asking his wages; but the boy is only whipped all the harder and kept penniless longer after Don Quixote leaves. The Don's "good turn" in reality has been a show of ego; he has flouted the ego of the boy's master, who takes that frustration also out on the poor servant. His liberal impulses induce him to free the king's prisoners whom he meets in chains on the road headed for the galleys. But society must punish its criminal violators of the norm in order to preserve its structure; these men, after stoning the Don who has aided them, run away and cause pain to society by their further crimes. One Gines of Passamonte in particular (he is also a writer!) gives Don Quixote trouble throughout his journeys. While he is wandering, his estates in Mancha languish. All his violations of other members of the society he excuses for himself according to the knightly code; when he has stolen a barber's brass basin (which he sees as a knight's helmet), Sancho Panza makes his excuse to the barber:

> "Thou liest," quoth Sancho; "for I am not a robber by the highways, for my Lord Don Quixote won these spoils in a good war."

On the wonderful road, all those whom Don Quixote meets are either nonprobable pariahs—whores, peddlers, thieves—or those who make a business of serving the traveler, or probable people in a temporarily nonprobable condition. These last are most numerous as lovers who have taken to a life of pastoral lamentation for a lost beloved. Don Quixote interests himself deeply in their plight because he can identify his own love with theirs. But they gain their marriage and reunite with society without his help. While the Don in his travels with these men becomes increasingly deluded and idealistic and incurs increasing pain, they successfully adjust themselves to the society once more. While social life resiliently adjusts itself around him, the Don adamantly continues in his fixed idea.

The aristocratic knight, who sought for the wonderful grail and individually redressed wrongs, nourished a love equally nonprobable; it depended on spiritual attraction to the aristocratic norm, could neither occur nor culminate in the married state, and lasted only so long as physical sex was absent. Chaucer showed the nonprobability of courtly love by contrasting the wonderful pact of eternal fidelity between Troilus and Cressida with the probable norm that an unattached woman will take a lover. Diomede is not a black character; his actions are those of any probable young man with an unmarried woman to whom he is attracted. While the lovers around him marry, Don Quixote ventures painfully through the world in search of Dulcinea del Toboso, the maiden to whom he vows faithfulness till death. Though at the beginning of his adventures he lusted for Maritornes at the inn, in the Second Part he rejects again and again the open advances of women in the Duke's castle. In a trip to Toboso he finds his Dulcinea to be an ugly country wench riding on a donkey; she must be enchanted, he concludes—like everything from inns to barber's basins that concretely contradicts the Don's idealism. While the other lovers are joining and marrying, Don Quixote is "naked to his shirt, lean, yellow, almost dead of hunger, and fighting for his lady Dulcinea." He dies without speaking to her.

Sancho Panza, the plebeian squire who accompanies the aristocratic-bourgeois Don Quixote, is also errant from probability, though he continually quotes proverbs (the social wisdom of the probable). As the Don searches for the wonderful, Sancho wants to change his probable lot on earth from tilling the soil to governing men. At first the adventures of the two are desperately unsuccessful, but the force of their persistence finally carries them into a measure of social success. In the Second Part they continually meet knights and noblemen who are acquainted with Don Quixote; a few even claim to be his old friend or to have started him on his quest.

A Duke who entertains the Don and Sancho in his home to trick them and feast them gives the island of Barataria to Sancho to govern. Sancho had already been warned by the probable wisdom of his wife Teresa that their lot was likely to remain the same till death. Far better, maintains Teresa, to marry our daughter Sanchica to a young fellow of her own station than to some aristocrat. She would only be miserable out of her station, like Molière's George Dandin. With a set of maxims by Don Quixote to guide him and his own homely folk wisdom, Sancho becomes a sage, popular, and just governor. The cases that come before him he judges like Solomon, or the ragged Azdak in Bertolt Brecht's *The Caucasian Circle of Chalk*. But Sancho finds in the course of governing that, plagued with wars, plots on his life, and a physician who oversees his diet, he prefers life as a simple farmer:

> A sickle is better in my hand than a governor's sceptre. I had rather fill myself with a good dish of gaspachos than be subject to the misery of an impertinent physician, that would kill me with hunger. I had rather solace myself under the shade of an oak in summer . . . than lay me down to the subjection of a government in fine holland sheets and be clothed in sables. Fare you well, sir, and tell my lord the duke naked was I born, naked I am. I neither win nor lose.

The probability of the social classes in the status quo is best for the classes themselves; an attempt to change them only results in misery for all concerned.

As Don Quixote becomes madder and madder in his individualism, the society makes attempt after attempt to bring him back into the fold as an honest bourgeois. Strangers like the Duke merely play good-natured tricks on him, but the old members of his village constantly try to get him back. It was for his own good/their preservation that his niece and a servant girl burned his books after his first sally. As the Knight of the Looking Glass, Samson de Carrasco, a young bachelor of his town, fails to vanquish him and extract from him the promise to return home for a year. But later on in the Second Part, as the Knight of the White Moon he defeats the Don and makes him promise to abandon knighthood and to manage his farms.

The idealism of Don Quixote is not so easily quenched, however; like Ulysses, Mickey Mouse, and the young man in the folk rituals, he rebounds in his old ways. While remaining true to his promise (he must, by the knightly code!) to Samson Carrasco, he decides to espouse at home the other individualist-romantic ideal; he will become a pastoral shepherd!

> In this field we met the brave shepherdesses and the lusty swains that would have imitated and renewed the pastoral Arcadia, an invention as strange as witty; in imitation of which, if thou thinkest fit, Sancho, we will turn shepherd for the time that we are to live retired. I will buy sheep, and all the things fit for our pastoral vocation; calling myself by the name of the shepherd Quixotiz, and thou the shepherd Pansino. We will walk up and down the hills, through woods and meadows, singing and versifying, and drinking the liquid crystal of the fountains, sometimes out of the clear springs, and then out of the swift running waters . . . . the moon and stars, in spite of night's darkness [night the symbol for the wonderful], shall give us light; our songs shall afford us delight, and our wailing, mirth.

But his stay at home holds another destiny for Don Quixote. In the course of his journeys he becomes wiser and wiser, expressing ideas of increasing depth and good sense. At one point, after watching a traveling stage performance, he had made the same reflection as one of Shakespeare's wise comic characters:

> Why, the same thing happens in the comedy and theatre of this world, where some play the emperors, others the bishops, and lastly, all the parts that may be in a comedy; but in the end—that is, the end of our life—Death takes away all the robes that made them differ, and at their burial they are equal.

While he was alive and well (though bruised), no man could convince Don Quixote of his folly. But when he is sick and expectant of death, he returns to the fold of the probable at last:

> I possess now a free and clear judgment, and nothing overshadowed with the misty clouds of ignorance, which the continual reading and plodding through books of chivalry had overcast me withal . . . . I am no more Don Quixote de la Mancha, but rather Alonso Quixano, unto whom my honest and civil conversation hath heretofore appropriated the surname of Good. I am now a professed enemy to Amadis de Gaule and of all the infinite rabble of his race. Now are all the profane histories of errant chivalry hateful unto me; I now acknowledge my folly and perceive the danger whereinto the reading of them hath brought me. But now, by the mere mercy of my God, become wise at my own proper cost and charges, I utterly abhor them.

At the end of the human journey, he casts aside the folly of his ideals, and honestly faces his own delusion. So the old, rich in probable wisdom, look on their own lives and those of the young around them as deluded by chimeras. To comedy, where social man lives as best he can in the mechanical struggle for survival, all idealism is folly, all individualism the unpardonable social sin. To the comic writer all men, insofar as they partake of the search for the wonderful, are Don Quixotes.

FIELDING

Most comic writers expel the pariah from society in sterility and disgrace. The benign Fielding, believing that merit is probably rewarded by society on this earth, restores his outcasts into the bosom of normal life. The pariah bastard Tom Jones, though he is harrowed by all manner of misfortune at the hands of prigs and scoundrels, is rehabilitated to the norms, marries the chaste and wealthy Sophia, and prospers normally by the fruit of his own good deeds. Squire Allworthy, the genial, omnipotent stepfather, may temporarily be deceived by the hypocrisy of a Tartuffe-like Blifil; in the end he is successful in knowing the norms of social action as they emerge, and he rewards everyone according to his deserts.

Tom Jones is represented at the beginning of the book as the bastard of Jenny Jones, a sensitive young girl who reads Latin and finds herself in that nonprobable situation more easily capable of departing from the norms of female conduct. Mrs. Wilkins the housekeeper and Squire Allworthy's sister want to cast the child on the parish, but the beneficent squire resolves to raise Tom himself. Nevertheless, the society continues to blame Tom for the abnormality of his birth, predicting a death by hanging for him each time he steals apples from a farmer's orchard or chases a rabbit on another's property. The social status of the generous Tom is contrasted with that of Master Blifil, the priggish legitimate son of Squire Allworthy's sister (who dies about fifteen years after her son's birth). The rift between the two symbolically comes to a head in the question of marriage, the crux of probable life. Squire Western's sister, desirous of making a good match for young Sophia Western, concludes from her proud knowledge (but actual ignorance) of the world that Sophia loves Master Blifil. Actually she loves Tom. Her refusal of her social equal, Blifil, creates dissension between the neighboring families, which results in eruption and flight. Tom Jones is cast forth into the world with the ill wishes of the "religious" Blifil and his partisan, the sadistic clergyman Thwackum.

As an outcast pariah, Tom decides he will go to sea, and heads for the Bristol road. He soon becomes involved with the harsh probability of being a stranger. He is cajoled for his money by innkeepers and almost induced to enlist in the army (the official refuge for the outcast, like the sea); fortunately a scuffle with the soldiers and some officers dissuades him from this enterprise. Like Oedipus, his flight from home brings him into the presence of one who is supposedly his real father, the pedantic Partridge, in whose domicile Jenny Jones had lodged, and who had been expelled from the community for seducing her. With his new companion, he continues to wander, meeting like Don Quixote many other outcasts on the road—women of easy virtue, robbers, and the misanthropic "Man on the Hill," who has withdrawn completely from society into contemplation.

Sophia, like Anna in *Man and Superman* and the modest young ladies in Gilbert and Sullivan, pursues her own design—the propagation of the race—with cold-blooded selfishness, though the strictest decorum. It was she who originally had kindled the spark of love in Tom; he had been indifferent to her at a time when she was completely enamoured of him. With her maid she takes flight from home, ostensibly away from marriage with Blifil, but actually in search of Tom. It is not long before she arrives at the inn where he is lodging. However, the excusable natural passions of Tom have led him into the bed of a lady who has given him much encouragement. Sophia cannot be other than outraged when she discovers this, and after making overtures to him by sending her muff to his bed, she departs in a flurry to London. As in *Pierre,* the wanderer in the country becomes an even greater outcast in the city; when Tom Jones pursues Sophia there, he meets all manner of constraining circumstances, and ends up as the gigolo of Lady Bellaston, with whom Sophia is staying.

The vital activity of the younger generation has likewise drawn all the older people to London. Squires Allworthy and Western, his unmarried sister Mrs. Western, and Master Blifil all arrive there to restore Sophia to an apparently normal social life. But the bourgeois appearance of norm in the hypocritical Blifil is no match for the natural reality of norm in Tom Jones. While demurely doing nothing forward and appearing to be an obedient daughter, Sophia firmly refuses both Blifil and the rough gallant, Lord Fellamar.

Mrs. Waters, the woman whom Tom had slept with at the inn, had run away with Lieutenant Fitzpatrick. When Tom meets this gentleman on the street, he engages in a duel with him, wounds him, and like

Pierre is sent to languish in prison. At the false report that Fitzpatrick's wound was mortal, Tom in complete disgrace awaits the sentence of death. He seems to have reached the nadir of misfortune. But Partridge uncovers the even more hideous fact that Mrs. Waters is Jenny Jones herself; Tom has therefore slept with his own mother! The deep guilt of the Oedipus myth descends on his head as he plumbs the bottom of pariahism. He had first been attracted to Mrs. Waters by the whiteness of her full, maternal breasts; and his imprisonment followed from a sword duel (phallic symbol) with Fitzpatrick (Laius), the ostensible murder of one who had fulfilled the office of husband to his supposed mother.

The plot motif of *Tom Jones* is identical with that of *Oedipus Rex:* A young man, raised by foster parents, runs away when he grows up: on the road he attacks a stranger who is his father. (But in *Tom Jones* Laius is split into Partridge and Fitzpatrick.) Then he marries his mother. In the search for the murderer of his father, he becomes an outcast. Finally, the full horor of his incest descends upon him. But while Oedipus the king probes the horrible implications of his wonderful guilt, comedy ritually recoils from the extreme situation by proving that the accusation is a false appearance.

It turns out—not too convincingly—that Squire Allworthy's sister had actually been the mother of the boy, who is at once freed of these charges and seen in the true light of his aristocratic birth. Blifil, who was informed of this by the scheming lawyer after his mother's death, deliberately hid the fact that Tom was his brother in order to gain a larger portion of Squire Allworthy's heritage. When events are pushed to the extreme of unfairness, the reality emerges beneath the appearance, and there is always at least one wise person on hand to recognize it.

All the facts have come into a true and normal light at the end of the book. The honest are rewarded by life and the unjust punished. After the comic author/audience has torn the veil off the pretensions and greediness of all society, the health of the normally generous remains. Squire Allworthy bestows his blessing of financial and social approval on Tom, whereupon he takes up the formal courtship of Sophia. Though she is

149

wounded in ego by his sexual infidelity, an appeal to her own image in a mirror suffices to win her. She must have her revenge by postponing the marriage, till the importunity of her father allows her to marry Tom the next day. As an obedient daughter, of course, she cannot do other than acquiesce. So they raise a family, and the novel ends with everyone who deserves it in fertile prosperity.

Tom's besetting error is not moral sin (which, like all men, he probably commits) but lack of prudence, a violation of the philosophy of the mean. Squire Allworthy says to him:

> You now see, Tom, to what dangers imprudence alone may subject virtue (for virtue, I am now convinced, you have in a great degree). Prudence is indeed the duty which we owe to ourselves; and if we will be so much our own enemies as to neglect it, we are not to wonder if the world is deficient in discharging their duty to us; for when a man lays the foundation of his own ruin, others will, I am afraid, be too apt to build upon it . . . . Remember them [imprudent acts] only yourself so far as for the future to teach you the better to avoid them; but still remember, for your comfort, that there is this great difference between them and those faults which can be deduced from villainy only:—The former, perhaps, are more apt to subject a man to ruin; but if he reform, his character will, at length, be totally retrieved; the world, though not immediately, will in time be reconciled to him . . . . But villainy, my boy, when once discovered, is irretrievable . . . . The censures of mankind will pursue the wretch, their score will abash him in public; and if shame drives him into retirement, he will go to it with all those terrors with which a weary child, who is afraid of hobgoblins, retreats from company to go to bed alone . . .

Fielding's magistrate's view of the world strips off all masks. He piles up a load of evidence, circumstances, actions of mixed motive, in his characters, that are worthy of a file of legal case histories. The inferences, conclusions, invectives, false interpretations which are wilfully or unwilfully put by society on the action as it progresses would stagger a Kafka. Yet this inextricable maze of good and evil, fact and fiction, truth and falsehood, is threaded in the course of time by the norms of social health.

The naturally good man (Tom Jones, Joseph Andrews) and the naturally good woman (Sophia, Amelia) will be rewarded, while the villain will be shunned, by society. The basic opposition in Fielding's work is between the villain triumphant/thwarted and the honest imprudent gulled/rewarded.

The priggish hypocrite, Blifil, goes so far as to plot to bribe criminals to testify against Tom when he is in prison, so that Tom will be put out of the way as his rival for love and fortune. Thwackum, the moralizing clergyman, hides his selfishness and sadism behind the mask of casuistry. The pattern of *Tom Jones* and Fielding's other novels is that of the temporary victory of plotting hypocrites, abetted by greedy servants and ignorant egotists, into power over the honestly imprudent. In the emerging norms of social experience, those who are imprudent learn the probable and those who have consistently performed villainies are discovered.

Fielding states at the beginning of *Tom Jones* that his purpose is "to laugh mankind out of their favorite follies and vices." Likewise in *Joseph Andrews,* which parodies Richardson's *Pamela* as *Tom Jones* parodies the epic, the good and honest young man is discovered to be the son of a lord in the nick of time; Joseph Andrews is rescued from the sexual assaults of Lady Booby, cleared of an incest charge with his supposed sister Fanny, and installed in a comfortable rural estate. He marries Fanny and lives in new affluence with his discovered father, the book ending as Fanny is big with child.

While the prigs and snobs in Fielding affect to be higher than the honest men and loathe vagabonds, in *Tom Jones* and *Jonathan Wild* the king of a gypsy or savage tribe is shown to know the nice distinctions of probable wisdom. It is a kind peddler who twice relieves Joseph Andrews and finally bears the news of his true birth. Parson Adams, low in the wealth of the world, is represented as utterly honest and good; only his lack of social, pure-action wisdom prevents him from acquiring the money which his more prudent wife would desire.

Fielding as a probable comic writer shows some sympathy for pure-action knowledge. He professes that the blunt Squire Western, though he had "not read Machiavel," nevertheless knew how to govern men.

151

If a good man is not rewarded, Fielding hints, as in the case of Parson Adams he must blame his own lack of knowledge of the world's ways.

> And here, in defiance of all the barking critics in the world, I must and will introduce a digression concerning true wisdom, of which Mr. Allworthy was in reality as great a pattern as he was of goodness. To say truth, the wisest man is the likeliest to possess all worldly blessings in an eminent degree; for as that *moderation* [italics mine] which wisdom prescribes is the surest way to useful wealth, so can it alone qualify us to taste many pleasures. The wise man gratifies every appetite and every passion, while the fool sacrifices all the rest to pall and satiate one.
>
> True wisdom, then, notwithstanding all which Mr. Hogarth's poor poet may have writ against riches, and in spite of all which any rich, well-fed divine may have preached against pleasure, consists not in the contempt of either of these. A man may have as much wisdom in the possession of any affluent fortune as any beggar in the streets; or may enjoy a handsome wife or a hearty friend, and still remain as wise as any sour Popish recluse, who buries all his social faculties, and starves his belly while he well lashes his back.

Yet Fielding continually expostulates against the absolute and excessive application of that wisdom for abnormal selfishness.

> This gentleman . . . was what they call a man of the world; that is to say, a man who directs his conduct in this world as one who, being fully persuaded there is no other, is resolved to make the most of this.

Avoiding the miser's sole regard for money, a man in society should preserve a golden mean of balance between the desires of his neighbors and his own self-interest.

Of all the undesirable characters in Fielding—slavish servants, snobs, lustful and hypocritical ladies, prudes and prigs, stupid pedants who abet the aristocracy, insensitive men of affairs—none is worse than the Machiavellian. In *Jonathan Wild,* Fielding ironically parallels pure-action politics with thievery (called "priggism" throughout as a pretended slang term). The underworld serves in irony as a symbol for the world of political manipulation. Goodness and greatness are incompatible; only a milksop

152

has any regard for honesty, humanity, or concern for anything other than his own interest:

> For these [writers], from their fear of contradicting the obsolete and absurd doctrines of a set of simple fellows, called, in derision, sages or philosophers, have endeavoured, as much as possible, to confound the ideas of greatness and goodness; whereas no two things can possibly be more distinct from each other; for greatness consists of making all manner of mischief on mankind, and goodness in removing it from them.

Comparing his thief with Alexander and Caesar, Fielding follows the career of this great man through his boyhood frauds and robberies into a full-fledged career of crime. When one of Jonathan Wild's underlings wants the possession of what he himself has stolen, the great man draws examples from the world of affairs to confute him:

> It is well said of us, the higher order of mortals, that we are born only to devour the fruits of the earth; and it may be as well said of the lower class, that they are born only to produce them for us.
>
> Is not the battle gained by the sweat and danger of the common soldier? Are not the honour and fruits of the victory the general's who laid the scheme? Is not the house built by the labour of the carpenter and bricklayer? Is it not built for the profit only of the architect, and for the use of the inhabitant, who could not easily have placed one brick upon another? ... Cast your eye abroad, and see who is it lives in the most luxurious buildings, feasts his palate with the most luxurious dainties, his eyes with the most beautiful sculptures and delicate paintings, and clothes himself in the finest and richest apparel; and tell me ... why then should the state of a prig (a thief) differ from all others?

This agent of the devil ruins an honest tradesman, Mr. Heartfree, who falls in prison, loses his wife, and finally is condemned to death by the machinations of Wild. Society, however, as is probable, finds out his villainy in the course of time. Wild's quarrel with his henchman Fireblood, who has intrigued with Wild's wife, brings about the discovery of these things; a wise magistrate (like Squire Allworthy—and Fielding himself), the agent of social will, rescues Heartfree as he is about to be condemned to death. His wife on all her travels on the sea, having first been led astray by Wild in the hope of helping her husband, preserves her chastity, has her jewels restored, and gets home by the success of generous men in society over those who have plotted her downfall. As Wild is hung, so the honest Heartfree becomes a prosperous merchant, the lesson being that only the normal are happy on this earth. Among the Machiavellis, even Alexander and Caesar, the extremes of pure-action genius, must die a violent death. The comedian penetrates the nature of pure action and emerges with the knowledge that social norms are good and healthy. Wild in the end has both "greatness" and death.

> Jonathan Wild had every qualification necessary to form a great man. As his most powerful and predominant passion was ambition, so nature had, with consummate propriety, adapted all his faculties to the attaining those glorious ends to which this passion directed him. He was extremely ingenious in inventing designs; artful in contriving the means to accomplish his purposes, and resolute in executing them; for as the most exquisite cunning and most undaunted boldness qualified him for any undertaking, so was he not restrained by any of those weaknesses which disappoint the views of mean and vulgar souls and which are comprehended in one general term of honesty, which is a corruption of honosty, a word derived from what the Greeks call an ass. He was entirely free from those low vices of modesty and good-nature, which were the only qualities which absolutely rendered a man incapable of making a considerable figure in the world.

England in the eighteenth century was a stable society where rationalism reigned, both in the order of classes and the productions of literature. Whether savage like Swift, boisterous like Fielding and Smollett, or genteelly correct like Pope, the important writings of this period all belong in some phase of the comic tradition. Their tragedies, like the *Cato* of Addison, are dull because they are probable. The deepest figure of the period remains the satirist Swift. In France even the rebels were rationalists, like Voltaire and Rousseau; the romanticism of the latter being nonprobable in probable focus, like that of Shelley.

154

It is fitting that the profoundest writer of the probable in the twentieth century should have gone to an eighteenth-century philosopher for the basic conceptual scheme of his greatest work. Even so, the historical eras of the profound Vico are the most imaginative and nonprobable part of the structure of *Finnegans Wake*.

Joyce's life career is that of the satirist who revolts from a probable world which he understands too well, though only in probable terms. As a young man Joyce's inclinations were toward naturalism. The chief influence on him in literature was the probable Ibsen and in philosophy the probable Aristotle. He was fascinated by the logical, probable structure of Saint Thomas, while rejecting the wonderful faith on which it was founded. *Dubliners* examines social types psychologically—the stories are almost like key incidents in case histories—such as the analysis of occupational frustration or two boys' meeting a pariah homosexual. His two broadsheets, written in couplets against Ireland while he was in Europe, are consistently in the bitter satiric tradition. Attracted to society and to the structure of the church, he could neither accept the appearance/reality mask (as an honest bourgeois can), nor understand the wonderful faith of religion. In *A Portrait of the Artist as a Young Man*, the adolescent Stephen/Joyce rejects the salvation of the soul and punishment for sins, which he sees only in probable, rationalist terms. The probable logic and authoritarianism of the Church appealed to him, but he was unable to understand its wonderful essence.

As was discussed above, *Ulysses*, like all allegories, is a rationalist novel written from a probable point of view. Though *Finnegans Wake* has been called a supreme work of symbolism because of its incredibly wide scope and its dream-smelting narrative technique, it, too, is a rationalist and probable comic work. Its basic form is the folk motif, its style pun and parody, and its fundamental theme that in man–woman (family) and parent–children (generation) relationships, all is probable and sexually regenerative.

Finnegans Wake has been said to embrace all life. Actually it presents in probable focus the recurrence of individual–social life according to a probable pattern, in the female pole of love (regeneration, revolution, change) and the male pole of war (rivalry, conquest by the foreigner, conversion). The folk motif becomes history, and the multiple events in history arrange themselves according to the norms of folk motif. Allegorically, all ideas in the dream are related to all others; as in *Ulysses* it is a closed—though extremely wide—circle of reference. Ideas belong to a particular member of a particular generation, and they will recur again as the property of the same types in history. The ultimate meaning of life is the pure action of sexual and social life course, birth through death. Death itself is seen only in the probable earthly terms of the wake, where death and life occur simultaneously; Shem and Shaun, the next generation, live on to inherit the characteristics of HCE.

The conquering Norwegian stranger, the sailor of the seas, the dead man, the dream—these wonderful facts are explained as a probable and predictable part of the recurring social insemination. In the "Triv and Quad" chapter, mathematical reasoning and diagrams are used to explain the polarities. Paradox is resolved not in the supralogical faith of the soul, as in a deep tragic work, but in the birth process of pure action that negates reason as mere speculation. The egotistical love of Tristan and Isolde is explained not as the yearning for the infinite of a young man and a young woman, but from a probable point of view as the lust of Father (identifying himself with son) for daughter. The nonprobable older, middle-aged man (Mark, Swift, HCE) desires his daughter of the younger generation (Isolde, Stella—or Vanessa, the two being interchangeable to Joyce). It is not the wonderful search of the ego for death/ultimate being, but the nonprobable crossing of generation norms. Original sin is seen in social, sexual terms—voyeurism and exhibitionism in a public park—not as the wonderful search/pride of the individual soul. And it belongs only to HCE, the male half of the duality, whose fall from innocence into guilt is simply a part of his male activity. Anna Livia Plurabelle, the female half, incurs not guilt, but physical dirt, experience, and age. Man learns in the world; woman only generates and mothers. The police power, the courts, public opinion, the failure of the nonprobable artist and his sexual ineptness, the army, sex, marriage—all the familiar probable topics of comedy absorb *Finnegans Wake*. The real meaning of death and guilt, optimistic or pessimistic tragedy, are foreign to its focus.

Joyce admired Dostoievsky and Jacobsen, and claimed that they were two important nineteenth-century influences on his writing. But one searches any of his books in vain for deep probing of the individual, any character who is more than a type. At times Joyce can be very dull, with the oppressive dullness of complete probability. All his characters are types, as much as if they were in a *commedia dell'arte*. Bloom, despite the elaborate documentation of his personal history, is merely a type, like HCE. Molly Bloom has been justly praised as an amazing portrait of the eternal woman; it has not yet been pointed out that she is nothing but the eternal woman, a social and sexual type portrayed in a probable document. The very method of *Finnegans Wake* strives to type the characters: ALP the mother, HCE the businessman-warrior father, Shem the pariah artist, Shaun the politician (the daughter is a one-dimensional portrait of ALP at an early age). A brief comparison of Joyce's entire repertoire of characters with those in Dostoievsky (how individual his women!) or even in Ibsen, will show to all but the most ardent enthusiast the comparative poverty of Joyce. He was a rationalist writer of satire and comedy, with an average imagination and an immense memory. His very writing career was a conscious act of will, like that of Flaubert. There shows in his choice of search no deep destiny, as with Shakespeare, Cervantes, Dostoievsky, Rimbaud, or even Henry Miller. The cast of *Finnegans Wake* is numerically staggering; when resolved into types, it emerges as very simple indeed.

Stylistically as well as in idea, motif, and character, *Finnegans Wake* belongs in the comic tradition. Its fertile pouring forth of myriad words, the probable documentation of a culture, is peculiar and typical to comedy, as Athenaeus and Richard Burton testify. The tragic writer never wallows in a catalogue and plethora of words, as students know who have compared the difficulty of Sophocles with that of Aristophanes, or the tragic parts of Shakespeare with the comic parts. In later times the comedian required far more abundant documentation and notes for his works

157

than the tragedian. Whereas almost anyone can read Montaigne, only the most accomplished can proceed rapidly through Rabelais. *Troilus and Cressida* is far easier than the *Canterbury Tales*. This orgy of language in a comic poet is at bottom another manifestation of the abnormal gluttony and suspension of mores that takes place in sex and feasting during the primitive comic ritual. It may also be explained as a reflection of the comedian's obsession with concrete, day-to-day, probable life. As with Rabelais, one justifiably associates Joyce's sexual amoralism (in his books) and implying of the norms with his unrestrained language.

In order to achieve multiple reference, the typing of many facts into a norm, *Finnegans Wake* utilizes far more extensively than any work in literary history the two comic techniques of punning and parody; the latter is hardly less pervasive than the former, and the two sometimes merge. *Finnegans Wake* abounds in parodied quotations of folk ballads, opera (*mild und leise*), mottos (*honi soit qui mal y pense*), personal journals (especially Swift's), newspaper writing, religious liturgy, philosophical discourse, hymns, political speeches, and tag ends of quotations from a dozen literary traditions.

The great quantitative extension of Joyce's factual knowledge, which he succeeds marvelously well in weaving into his novels, obscures the fact that he was neither abnormal nor profound in the creation of symbols. He is a Rabelais, but not a Shakespeare, or even an Eliot; the symbols in the *Waste Land* search a depth far beyond the powers of the writer of *Finnegans Wake*. Stunned by the number of words in his vocabulary, most critics tacitly acknowledge him to be the greatest of modern stylists. Though the subleties of rhythm in *Finnegans Wake* deserve much praise and command admiration, Joyce's feeling for word and symbol (the two are mutually dependent in a cultivated writer) was not extraordinary.

His choice of word, like the *mot juste* of probable Flaubert, is the rationalist search for the exact word, the physically descriptive and rhythmical term. Joyce never searches for the word which expresses deep symbolic relationships. To say nothing of Shakespeare and Dante, many modern poets within their more limited scope—Valéry, George,

158

Wallace Stevens, John Crowe Ransom—surpass Joyce in the feeling for and choice of words. He never tunes his words symbolically to produce the deep chords and chaste echoes that a number of modern writers have achieved. This becomes abundantly clear when he writes in a limited tradition, the short story or the conventional lyric. *Dubliners* is verbally flat compared with the early stories of Djuna Barnes, and, as Pound has seen, all his poems are mediocre exercises that could be turned out mechanically by anyone with some flair and practice in rhyme and metre. Style reflects a writer's depth and cast of mind; a rationalist will possess a mechanical style which no yearning for deep symbols can extend.

In all his writing Joyce is obsessed with the problem of the artist in society; in the satiric tradition his characters are not searchers for the wonderful (though in some of the critical conversations of *Ulysses,* Joyce seems to yearn for that); they are bitter rebels against society, outcasts abnormal vis-à-vis society, whose violation of the old norms is a necessary act in the change of cultural generation. Vico's scheme for the four parts of *Finnegans Wake* is carried out only in outward structure; the "theological" and "aristocratic" books, capable of wonderful treatment, are handled in a probable focus and are nearly indistinguishable from the other two books. God the Father is an anthropological fact, *natura naturans,* the oversoul of generative power so dear to philosophers of the probable. He is the sexual creator of the new in old patterns, the turner of the cyclic wheel (one thinks of probable Aristotle's "proof" of God as the originator of motion). The generation images in *Finnegans Wake* resemble more the lush *Pervigilium Veneris* or the lavish Rabelais than the mystic generation symbols in St. Theresa and Blake.

The themes that pervade *Finnegans Wake*—sex, politics, law, and war—are recurrent subjects for comedy and other probable thought. The Church is constantly parodied and revelation is seen as the beginning of a new, probable cycle. The basic allegorical associations are individual–society generation process, the body of the man being identified with the physical body of the town. Even the dream of the whole work is a probable dream of sexuality; there is little else of the Freudian in it, and certainly no individuality, which Freud, as quoted in Chapter II, saw as the focus of the dream-life. It is the dream of Leopold Bloom and James Joyce, not of Dante and Dostoievsky.

Finnegans Wake finds no parallel in modern literature. It is a magnificent comedy, perhaps the greatest of its type in all time. But it has rationalist limitations of style, character, action, and depth, which keep it out of the class of the less sensational *Odyssey* and *Tempest*. A social and probable comedy, it can rightly be called all-inclusive; it is far from being all-searching.

THE DARK VOYAGE AND THE GOLDEN MEAN
THE ODYSSEY AND *THE TEMPEST*

Consider the subtleness of the sea; how its most dreaded creatures glide under water, unapparent for the most part, and treacherously hidden beneath the loveliest tints of azure. Consider also the devilish brilliance and beauty of many of its remorseless tribes, as the dainty embellished shape of many species of sharks. Consider, once more, the universal cannibalism of the sea. . . .

Consider all this; then turn to this green, gentle, and most docile earth; consider them both, the sea and the land; and do you not find a strange analogy to something in yourself? For as this appalling ocean surrounds the verdant land, so in the soul of man there lies one insular Tahiti, full of peace and joy, but encompassed by all the horrors of the half known life. God keep thee! Push not off from that isle, thou canst never return!
— MOBY DICK

The note of banishment, banishment from the heart, banishment from home, sounds uninterruptedly from the Two Gentlemen of Verona *onward till Prospero breaks his staff, buries it certain fathoms in the earth and drowns his book. It doubles itself in the middle of his life, reflects itself in another, repeats itself, protasis, epistasis, catastasis, catastrophe. It repeats itself again when he is near the grave, when his married daughter Susan . . . is accused of adultery. . . . Age has not withered it. Beauty and peace have not done it away. It is in infinite variety everywhere in the world he has created, in* Much Ado

About Nothing, *twice in* As You Like It, *in the* Tempest, *in* Hamlet, *in* Measure for Measure, *and in all the other plays which I have not read.* —STEPHAN DEDALUS (JOYCE) ON SHAKESPEARE.

In the Odyssey *Homer may be likened to a sinking sun, whose grandeur remains without its intensity . . . there is not the same profusion of accumulated passions, nor the supple and oratorical style, packed with images. . . . You seem to see . . . the ebb and flow of greatness, and a fancy roving in the fabulous and incredible, as though the ocean were withdrawing into itself and were being laid bare within its own confines. . . . The fabulous* (μῦθος) *element, however, prevails throughout the poem over the real* (τὸ πρᾶκτικον) *. . . . . The genius of great poets and prose-writers, as their passion declines, finds its final expression in the delineation of character* (ἦθος). *For such are the details which Homer gives, with an eye to characterisation* (ἠθικῶς) *of life in the home of Odysseus; they form as it were a comedy of manners* (κωμῳδία ἠθολογουμένη). —LONGINUS

MIRANDA: *I am a fool*
         To weep at what I am glad of.
PROSPERO: *Faire encounter*
         Of two most rare affections: heavens raine grace
         On that which breeds betweene 'em.
FERDINAND: *Wherefore weepe you?*
                             —THE TEMPEST

The *Iliad's* tragedy has a systematic structure; in antinomic symbols—light—darkness, hero—king, society—individual, war—peace—it demonstrates the tragic probability of death incurred in the individual's most extreme social duty, service in war. Sarpedon and Glaucus discuss—Achilles must learn—that the honor they hold in society springs only from the value to society of their dangerous function as warriors. In war the net of social duty draws tight, and death becomes probable for the individual. "Like to the race of leaves is the race of mortal men." A blast of wind in the late autumn of a harsh war and they fall in numbers to the ground. Death and the meaning it sheds on individual/society is the basic theme of the *Iliad*. The countless slaughters of men, the *Iliad's* obsession with recounting the death of warriors in battle, which have offended many modern critics, are a justifiable background for a tragedy of which the central theme is death by duty. In anonymous social terms, the warriors who die are the probability against which we measure the predictable fate of Hector and Achilles.

Individual man in the *Iliad* is enmeshed in the ego-nexus of society. In Book I we enter at once the brutal social ethos of a tribe at war. The heroes flaunt themselves and are shocked against the egos of one another. A priest like Chryses is mercilessly taunted till he can bring power to bear on those who oppose him, and a satiric member of the lower classes like Thersites is beaten and mocked when he ventures to criticize his officers. Therein lies the meaning of social disgrace for man awaiting the loser of the war, the equivalent of the rape that stands imminent for the women of the vanquished.

In Book II the scope and tension of the dominating society widens with the pageant of the entire marching army under the generalship of Agamemnon. The probability of this social mass is aptly pointed up by the succession of beast similes. The army is compared to a flock of cranes, a swarm of bees, as a predictable mass whose members merge into the general impression of a whole. And it is the character of that mass as a whole that will determine the winner of the war by free will of power/fate of Zeus. We know that the bronze-clad warlike Achaeans must be victorious over the horse-taming long-gowned Trojans.

Hector is predominantly the social man, *qua* husband of Andromache and defender of the Trojans; so Agamemnon is valid socially *qua* general of the Achaeans and Achilles *qua* hero who slaughters the enemy. The individual hybris of these two is tragic in that it impedes the social function/ethical health of the character. Odysseus is seen *qua* wise counsellor, Helen *qua* attractive but baneful cause of the war, Nestor *qua* old man who has already performed his social function in the probable maturity of a previous generation and is therefore entitled to respect. Achilles in the course of his wrath and its social consequence, the death of his friend, is brought to the individual knowledge of his limits as a man in society. He is not a god, but a mortal who must die in battle as a consequence of earning glory. Abnormally early death is the condition of his abnormal prowess. And he learns that his value is not pure and shining idea, the absolute virtue of an individual soul; it varies with the social function he performs: when he becomes enraged and ceases fighting, the honor derived from that gradually slackens. Society, to which he is bound, must suffer—and ultimately he must himself suffer as a member of that society, which is symbolized by the death of Patroclus.

That the individual is tragically enmeshed in the fate of his society and duties is symbolized in the *Iliad* by the systematic structure, the completely interrelated nexus of antinomic symbols. The active hybris of godlike Achilles contrasts with the passive hybris of ruling Agamemnon. And the brilliance of Achilles is also seen in intimate connection with the state of his own knowledge, the Achaean society, Hector as competent husband, or anything else. Light–darkness, Trojan–Achaean, warring man–loving woman, honor–disgrace, old Nestor–young Diomede, bourgeois Odysseus–satiric Thersites, lover Paris–husband Menelaus, wifely Andromache–mistress Helen, and so on. The structure—which John Finley has compared to a diamond—is symbolic, therefore in infinitely multiple contrast; unending antinomic associations can validly be called forth at will: Hector–Helen, Hector–Hecuba, Priam–Agamemnon, Agamemnon–Menelaus, servants–Helen, old men–Helen, old men–

servants, charioteers–bowman, killer–killed, coward–hero. Everyone and everything partakes of some facet, therefore, in focus, the whole of society. The association pattern is endless because in individual symbolic terms every man implies all other men. Achilles, though his probable character is active hybris, even has a touch of passive hybris, because each man contains in himself the germ of all sins.

The systematic structure of the tragic *Iliad,* portraying social duty and individual death, contrasts the experiential structure of the comic *Odyssey,* portraying the pure-action *Wanderjahre* of the family man returning to sexual union and the social power of his home kingdom. Both Aristotle and Longinus see in the *Odyssey* a comedy of manners (ἦθος).

As the *Iliad* explored the implications of the tragic individual by placing him in a social focus, the *Odyssey* shows the social man in individual focus. The symbolic relationships of the *Iliad* are infinitely complex; in the *Odyssey* everyone is grouped around the central figure. Telemachus is seen only as Odysseus' son, Penelope as *his* wife, whose suitors outrage *him.* Eumaeus is *his* swineherd, Laertes *his* father, Eurycleia *his* nurse. All other symbolic relationships are valid only in relation to the central figure. Laertes–Penelope or Penelope–suitors, even Penelope–Telemachus or Telemachus–Nestor, have symbolic validity in relation to Odysseus, but not otherwise.

Odysseus is the social man from the selfish, hedonistic point of view of his mannered experience (fate, reason, comedy). He undergoes fortunes, builds character (ἦθος, which Aristotle defined as the probable accumulation of acts into a group of habits), amasses knowledge. Hector, on the other hand, is social man in ethical religious duty. He is a warrior for the Trojans, not a crafty counsellor. His function as husband is to fertilize his wife and give her a social position which she and her son lose when Hector dies. Odysseus reflects the pleasurable, selfish side of marriage, the joy of its habit, the bond of sexual custom between husband and wife. When Hector returns to Troy before battle, he occupies himself with young Astyanax as well as with Andromache, but when Odysseus finds Penelope (as is probable in comedy through

165

Shaw, who shows it in *Candida*), they leave their son and proceed to bed—not for new children, presumably, but for their own pleasure. Odysseus is predominantly the wedded lover (hedonism, comedy), Hector the father of Andromache's children (duty, tragedy). Penelope's fortunes and position seem to be secure. She thinks primarily of her individual loss in companionship with the death of Odysseus. Andromache grieves with Hector's death over her social demise into slavery and the crippling of Astyanax' potentialities as a leader. Her fate is linked to that of the defeated social group in the war. Penelope, a member of a comic family, can probably remain safe and succeed, whatever happens to a particular social group.

Odysseus is not the wise governor of men like Agamemnon, Priam or Menelaus, but a pure-action diplomat. The government of men in its own terms is an aristocratic ideal (tragic); diplomacy, a pure-action technique (comic). Odysseus is no king at the head of a great social body, but the overlord of a single lonely island inhabited by the shepherds and farmers of a country gentry who keep pretty much to themselves. His position is more like that of a modern rancher than that of a mayor. Even at Troy his social position is not equal to that of the other rulers. He is a provincial noble, a courtier from beyond the seas who, according to one legend, had originally dodged the levy of warriors and had to make his way among the other aristocrats, as a bourgeois businessman does, by sleight of diplomacy. The individuality of the modern rancher is a cliché of psychological case histories; the relation of Odysseus to his herds is that of rancher to his cowboys, hard aloof interest with a commercial basis, quiet superiority. Penelope and Odysseus are not the only cultivated and wealthy inhabitants of the island, but they do not belong to an urban society like that of Lacedemon. Their social life is like that of the rancher who occasionally visits other ranchers but is largely preoccupied with managing his uncouth underlings. Odysseus' sympathy for the former nobility of his swineherd could be paralleled on a dozen ranches. As a commander of ships he more closely resembles the lonely commander of the *Pequod* and the *Sea-Wolf,* than the admiral of a national navy, except that these characters are tragic failures and he is a comic success, which makes them considerably less social and merry than Odysseus.

Wonderful war, always a failure in social terms, can produce success for the individual through trying his soul with nonprobable sufferings, hardening it by fire. When the storm scatters the Grecian heroes and they make their way toward the horizon of their own probable homes from the wonderful battle, Odysseus, longest of all on the seas, can be said to have profited most from his war service. His twenty years in exile ripened him and deepened his perceptions. The comic hero cannot fail; he will twist all into success. As probable Joyce said, "The artist can make no mistakes; his errors are the portals of discovery."

In the harmony of Greek society, where Apollo the god of probable success was also the god of art, the individual did not have to retreat from society to explore the wonderful. The result was an harmonious but delimited art. So Odysseus in his enriching travels learns from the *Wanderjahre*. A comic Faust, he does not have to lose his soul to the devil, as Dante on the threshold of Faustian civilization represents him, in order to make his explorations. In our civilization, on the other hand, it is the creative intellectual, the man apart from society, who can learn from exploration. Odysseus is not that, but a social man, the individual hedonist in a comic, social perspective who eats, drinks, makes love in play and is a manager and diplomat by calling. All these activities are nonprobable for a Faust.

For fundamental reasons explored in Spengler's writings but too complicated to discuss at length here (see especially *Decline of the West*, English translation, I, 326-28), Western-European literature is esoteric and unpopular, Greek literature exoteric and popular. Our type of the searcher must therefore be the nonprobable scholar, Faust, not the bourgeois Odysseus. It is just this difference in civilizations which makes Odysseus the diplomat so interesting as a searcher and Bloom the salesman so dull. Conversely, Telemachus is dull and his analogue Stephen, interesting. The searcher as *l'homme moyen sensuel,* at the core of Greek society, does not come off in Western-European art. Bloom is unconvincing without the creative powers of a Hamlet, a Lear, a Prospero.

167

He and HCE are both plastic, both intensely documented—but to little effect. Because of the difference in cultures, an attempted analogue to the *Odyssey* like *Ulysses* which follows faithfully the outward characteristics of the Odysseus myth cannot be analogous. *The Tempest,* whose protagonist is a Faustian magician, is the true analogue for the *Odyssey* in our culture.

Both ancient and modern commentators agree that the *Odyssey* is a comedy of manners. It has many of the superficial features of comedy and often breaks into outright jokes. Most of the Phaeacians' names are puns of nautical terms, and Monro notes several other linguistic jokes, puns, misappropriation of epithets, and the like. In the presentation of the bards Phemius and Demodocus, with his lavish praise of the poetic function, Homer seems to violate the third-person epic convention. One of Demodocus' lays—the cuckolding of Hephaestus by Ares and Aphrodite—is straight comedy.

The language of the *Odyssey,* like that of Rabelais and Joyce, is fertile in specific terms, but not nearly so rich in symbols as the *Iliad*—a fact so striking that some nineteenth-century scholars wanted to use it as a basis for comparative dating of the epics. Some of the intense symbols of the *Iliad* are curiously modern, such as the comparison of Greek captains to lions in the night (recalling Rousseau's *Sleeping Gypsy*), or Hector's flight from Achilles to the unending flight in a dream. The language of the *Odyssey* and its symbols, like those in *The Tempest* and *Moby Dick,* abound in a wealth of natural detail. The veil of symbolism is much thinner under the sun of comedy than in the dark antinomies of the tragic night.

E. A. Havelock rightly interprets the actions of the gods on Olympus in the *Iliad* as a domestic comedy, which is at the same time a skeptical debunking of the immortals and a representation of the normal peacetime life of the Grecian warriors. It is profoundly significant that the spirit of these comic interludes is probable and rationalistic; but as soon as the gods function in the tragic passages of war, the main action of the epic, they become wonderful, imaginative, and all-powerful. In his probable and rationalist comic relief the poet regards them skeptically;

in his tragedy, he has faith in them. Only the probable–wonderful (reason–faith, comedy–tragedy) antinomy can explain this contradiction in treatment of the gods in the *Iliad* which has puzzled so many modern critics.

The comedy of the *Iliad* is relief, like the interludes in *Lear* or *Hamlet.* The *Odyssey,* like *The Tempest,* is a serene comedy, and it views the gods throughout with a faint rationalist skepticism. Butler called it the "mild irreverence of the vicar's daughter." Compare the tone of the masque in *The Tempest.*

Returning home after their victory over the Trojans, the Greek heroes were scattered afar for further adventures by a god-sent storm. Their most adroit probable diplomat remained longest on the seas—twenty years exploring the wonders and miracles of the semi-divine lands he visited. The desire of his own free will and probable intelligence (the aid of Athene) yearned to reënter the ruts of his familial life, but the ambiguity of his will, the fate of the gods, and the hostility of the wonderful sea (Poseidon) kept him on his searching voyage. In his willed/fated search of the wonderful/return homeward, the paths at home, untrod by his foot for years, grew up with fat weeds. Suitors besieged his wife Penelope, whom she passively endured as a woman (perhaps also flattered by their attentions), but would not marry. Telemachus grew up abnormally under the hostility of the suitors rather than normally under the benevolence of his father. Odysseus' own father, Laertes, lived bitterly in a filthy hut and his old dog Argos lay feebly upon a heap of dung.

The popularity and richness of the inserted tale which he tells under the misty aura of the past to the Phaeacians has obscured the fact that Odysseus' return home is the absorbing theme of the *Odyssey,* even more than the restitution of Prospero in his dukedom absorbs the action of *The Tempest.* Over half the books are set in Ithaca itself.

The arrival in Phaeacia is analogous to arrival in Ithaca. Odysseus' introduction to probable family life in Phaeacia is exquisitely sweet because it is not roughened by the poignance and hardness of the past, as is the return to Ithaca. He meets the young princess Nausicaa, not his old

169

swineherd Eumaeus; is conducted to a palace, not to a hut, and contests playfully with nobles in an athletic contest rather than with a beggar in a bloody fight. The king gives him gifts, and he could culminate his joy there—as must have taken place in the self-enclosed folk motif which is archetypal to this incident—by marrying Nausicaa. The princess herself expects no less. But the genius of Homer has translated the wishful romance of folk motif into the wide reality of life. The past, as it must, urges Odysseus homeward from the unreal islands where he lingers. The tug of the emotional habits of marriage, the strongest of human ties, is woven into his flesh and the texture of his mind. (Penelope's flesh realistically warms at her husband's return.) More natural and probable than the heedlessly searching Ulysses of *Inferno* XXVI who had abandoned his home and sailed beyond the pillars of Hercules, he considers his deepening adventures as obstacles in the path of his constantly desired goal. Proud Agamemnon, whose family is contrasted throughout by both gods and men as the standard analogy to Odysseus', has not been so fortunate/wise. (As Monro remarks, folly and misfortune are linked in the *Odyssey;* we are probably to blame for our own ills.)

Odysseus weeps as Demodocus sings of the Achaeans. He reveals himself to Alcinous and begins to tell the wondering members of the strange court the discoveries of his tempestuous travels. The religious motifs of the deep racial past and the voyages of Greek travellers to far lands (there are even traces of icebergs in the Odyssey!) have poured into the common stream of the poet's knowledge of the wonderful and formed the stuff of the imaginative voyage. After a few years Odysseus has sailed in sight of his native island; but the folly of his comrades greedily induces them to open Aeolus' bag of winds. Almost at once he meets the gross giant Polyphemus, and the wonders grow deeper and deeper as he progresses, till finally he visits the realm of death itself. In that land, when their shades have drunk of the black blood in the pit, Tiresias the prophet, his mother Eurynome, Agamemnon (still spiteful), Ajax, Achilles, and his dead comrade Elpenor speak to him or pass by. The heroes of legend, Orion and Heracles, and finally legendary sinners against the gods, Sisyphus, Tityon, and Tantalus pass before his eyes.

His fear unfulfilled that dread Persephone, queen of the underworld, would freeze him with a Gorgon's head, Odysseus makes his way back again to the island of Circe, who had first directed him to Hades. The final trials of the Sirens, and Scylla and Charybdis are evaded only by Odysseus. His comrades have grossly partaken of the Oxen of the Sun, and perish on the sea for their sin. Only the leader himself, the type of successful hero, is washed half-dead onto the rocks of Phaeacia.

During his unpredictable roaming of twenty years, Odysseus' gaze was always toward his home and his wife. On Calypso's isle while the nymph lay in the shady cave surrounded by poplars and sea birds, Odysseus sat all day long on the rocks looking out to the barren sea. Not even the enticement of wonderful immortality could induce him to give up his return, so strong is the tug of the probable past. Once back at Ithaca, however, he must clear out the weeds that have grown up in his absence. When he poses as a strange beggar, it is probable that he would clash with the town beggar Iros in brutal fighting. The dog alone, true to his old habits, can recognize his master; all the human beings on the island have so created other probabilities that they fail to remember their chieftain under the beggar's guise which Athene has cast over him. Struck at first by lonely homesickness, he bitterly accepts the knowledge of the island as it had become. It is inevitable that, to clear out the upgrowth, he must slay the probable suitors of his wife. Once having gained his revenge and cleared his way by their slaughter, his wife—the heart and symbol of his return—is the last one who remains to be won over. A reference to the tree which forms their bedpost, a symbol of the probable, as in the lines from Yeats' *Prayer For My Daughter*:

> *Ceremony's a name for the rich horn,*
> *And custom for the spreading laurel tree*

at last proves him her genuine husband. They repair to bed.

The last book, like a nineteenth-century English novel, ties up the final strings in probable success. The suitors arrive in Hades to converse with the still-grieving Agamemnon. Odysseus searches out Laertes, reveals himself after teasing his old father a bit, and quiets the last skirmishes of the Ithacans after the neighboring families of the suitors have come to bury their dead. Still there remains the long journey before his death, laid on him by Tiresias, the trip inland to found a tomb to Poseidon. As the *Iliad* leaves off at the probable return of Hector's body to Priam with the unfulfilled death of Achilles in probable imminence, so the *Odyssey* leaves the probability of the hero's life shaded with the necessary last voyage, symbolic/actual death. The return home of Odysseus is the renewal of the aged Homer's faith in life.

THE TEMPEST

Home, the nest that warms from the gathered rags of our habits, is type and symbol of the probable in life. And voyage, spatial change in the cosmos that brings novelty to the traveler's eye, is symbol for the wonderful. In their symbolic fertility, home and voyage suggest the related antinomy land–sea, set forth in the quotation from Melville at the head of this chapter. The sea itself can be explored in various imaginative ways. The tragic novelist Melville created an absolute spatial symbol for the wonderful, the white whale, as counter to the relative temporal symbol, the sea. The lonely and unhappy Ahab ventures in his own free will toward the utter whiteness of the whale, the certainty of his own violent death. Prophetic Pip the good angel, Starbuck the religious social man both warn him away, and even the black angel, Parsee Fedallah, who himself as devil must fall in death by the same fate as Ahab, informs in advance his still free soul of the damnation he is choosing. The pains of his long years and the plotting and toil of the *Pequod's* long journey cannot be other than ineffectually relative against the destructive absolute. Meeting the pure wonderful entails destruction.

In the comic *Odyssey,* the social man ventures from home and returns home on the wonderful sea. The explorations of duty, war, geography, other kingdoms, and the supernatural wonders of the world, are only a preparation for the recurrent probable life. Ahab proceeds in time through the wonderful to absolute wonder (death). Odysseus proceeds in time through the wonderful back to his probable home. Prospero,

172

obliviously dwelling as outcast on a green isle of the wonderful sea, explores the wonder of magic in his pariah–king role, till he once more gains the power to harmonize family and kingdom.

G. Wilson Knight in *The Shakespearian Tempest* traces through all the plays the tempest–music antinomy. He suggests further related symbols, which can be tabled and grouped under the headings of this book's antinomy:

Dark Voyage	*Golden Mean*
tempest	music
beast (Caliban)	spirit (Ariel)
sea-winter	land-summer
discord	concord
rock[3]	jewel
war	love (peace)
thunder	harmony
death	birth-harvest

And I would add to this the probable day and wonderful night as basic symbols for all. One should think of the symbolic northern night that shrouds *Hamlet* and *Macbeth* in contrast to the clearly lighted day of *The Tempest.*

Lest we betray the imagination into taking this table as a mechanical allegory rather than fruitful symbol, let us remember that in *Antony and Cleopatra* the land (world, Rome) serves for war and the sea for love. (Still, in symbol's infinite suggestiveness, we might say that war-as-social-duty means concord for Antony, and love-as-wonderful-temptation, the tempestuous destruction of his life.)

A comparison between this table and those at the end of Chapters I and II will bring forth startling suggestions. The probable, sub-human beast of the earlier tables has shifted to the "wonderful" side, and superhuman spirit to the "probable"! Shakespeare's symbolism discovered by Knight clearly shows favor for the Golden Mean, which

---

[3] I make this addition to Mr. Knight's symbols, having in mind the caves of Wales in *Cymbeline*, the cliffs of Dover in *King Lear*, and so on.

Chapter I identifies with rationalism and probability. To explain this in terms of the previous discussion, we may say that Shakespeare's symbolism is not simple probability, but one of our transformations, the wonderful-as-probable (like Plato's Idea); and the Dark Voyage is an unselfconscious search for the nonprobable, while Prospero succeeds as a true searcher for the wonderful.

This difference between simple probability and wonderful-as-probable explains in clumsy dialectical language the superiority in tone and symbol of the *Odyssey* and *The Tempest* over the boisterous, mechanical comedy of Rabelais, Joyce, and Shakespeare's earlier plays. The great comedian creates symbols for the probable in Aristophanic comedy, satire, irony. The tragedian creates symbols for the wonderful. Only the transcendent figures of world literature can truly produce—others can smugly concoct —the serene, sublime comedy of wonderful-as-probable. Aged Homer, Dante, the author of the book of Tobit (with its little voyage), and Shakespeare in his last plays, have traveled through the storms of symbolic action into the calm of understanding.

Already in 1597 with *Henry IV, Part I,* Shakespeare had juxtaposed comic and tragic scenes in symbolic contrast to one another. As his perspective deepened and the tone of his plays richened, he explored varied types of comedy—the early serene fantasy of *Midsummer Night's Dream,* the salty irony of *Troilus and Cressida,* the bourgeois comedy of *Measure for Measure.* Comedy and tragedy, at first contrasted, came to be blended, as in the graveyard scene of *Hamlet* or the fool's speeches while wandering on the stormy heath with Lear. Even more completely were they fused in the final scene of *Antony and Cleopatra,* when the clown hands the defeated queen the basket of asps that will sting her to death. Finally, tragedy itself is purged from the imagination in a comic transcendence. Prospero foresees all plots, stupidities, the very worldviews of those who have landed on his island kingdom, and he manipulates them harmoniously for the common good.

The symbols of the characters, events, and places in *The Tempest,* like those in the voyage of Odysseus, immediately lend themselves to this or that allegorical interpretation. From the existential symbols of the play one can construct any number of valid referential allegories. One critic, for example, discovers Miranda as art; Prospero, old Shakespeare; Ferdinand, young Fletcher; his cutting of wood, the drudgery of learning the poetic craft, and so on. Speculation about Ariel and Caliban— one can make much of Shakespeare's care that they do not appear together— has been as great as that about Circe and the Sirens. We will ignore such possibly fruitful exploration of one thread in symbol to explore certain general features of the play. Outwardly, the characteristic features of comedy are there: success, happiness, disguises, the family, the marriage feast at the end. But like the *Odyssey, The Tempest* diverges from the conventional pattern. Usually in probable comedy the pattern is: abnormality of the pariah, his expulsion by normal society, the joy of society. In serene comedy of wonderful-as-probable (or vice versa), the pattern becomes: expulsion of the searcher (the culmination of a tragic play like *Lear, Hamlet, Richard II*), his experience in the wonderful, his self-rehabilitation with new knowledge into control of society. Prospero, like almost all Shakespeare's protagonists (see the Joyce quotation at the head of the chapter), undergoes the first stage. The later plays alone, *Winter's Tale, Cymbeline, Pericles,* include the third stage, return to harmony. Whether this is degeneration or maturing from the plays of the "tragic period" is an interesting but unanswerable question. It is enough to note that there is progression from probable comedy through tragedy to the serene comedy of wonderful-as-probable.

In one important element of its symbolic plot, *The Tempest* differs not only from the three other plays of reconciliation mentioned above, but also from any other comedy (or tragedy, except *Othello*) that comes to mind: *The central character himself, by the power of his wonderful magic in the patterns of probable wisdom, creates all the action of the play.* Shakespeare reminds us of this again and again. Prospero causes the tempest, wrecks the ship, spares the passengers and crew, induces the two plots of Antonio and Sebastian against Alonso and of Trinculo, Stephano and Caliban against himself. He kindles and fans the love between Miranda and Ferdinand, and gives them opportunity to see one another— as they think, secretly. Bringing the party from the ship at last within his magic circle, he himself causes in them the pangs of guilt necessary for him to pardon them. Tempest and music, exile and return, are the creations of his wand and book. True, Ariel is the agent of these miracles. But it was Prospero who had gained his bondage by the power, itself supernatural, to free him from the pine wherein Sycorax had prisoned him. The spirit could not stomach the witch's behests, but he has no difficulty, though chafing at confinement, in executing the commands of Prospero. He even seems to take a sportive delight in his work, not wholly to be explained by his expectation of coming freedom. In the new harmony of family and state, while chiding Miranda for seeing the "brave new world" with rosy eyes ("'tis new to thee"), he no longer needs his magic and scholarship. He breaks his wand and will drown his book "deeper than did ever plummet sound." In his success he can mold by his wonderful magic even the probable pure action of the courtiers who had cast him adrift on the sea after divesting him of his dukedom.

Almost a god symbol while retaining all personal features, Prospero may justly be called the queerest of Shakespeare's characters. Nor is he altogether likable. By his own fault he had been expelled from Milan. If he had not neglected his royal duties in favor of his library, his brother Antonio would never have been able to wrest the rule from him. Clearly he is a better ruler of the island than Sycorax had been. Yet he is not wholly exonerated from his harsh treatment of Caliban. That fishy monster had guided Prospero around the island, but the old man tyrannizes over him, allegedly for overtures of seduction to Miranda. Yet this understandable offense did not even come to the attempt at force. In a modern business such a proposal would not even be valid grounds for dismissing an employee. On the natural level of this play, which accepts life utterly as it is, Prospero's treatment of Caliban can be understood. And on the symbolic level it can be made to yield meaning. Only in abstract ethical terms, which are as foreign to comedy as they are indigenous to tragedy, can Prospero be condemned for his action.

The life-views of the other characters—the hasty pessimism of Sebastian, the Utopian optimism of Gonzago—clearly reflect the inner mind of the person, not the outward circumstances, which are alike for all. And they

176

are related to the capacity for unselfish love. Specifically, Gonzago is happier than Sebastian because his life has been kinder to others. The remorse necessary for purging evil to which Prospero's magic power brings these nobles bodes well for the lasting harmony of the state. The magic of Prospero has wrought not just a shift in power, which any diplomat could effect, but the permanent change of making the rulers understand themselves inwardly. The agency of wonderful magic is, however, only temporary. In the new harmony (a title taken for another modern Utopia), it will presumably be abandoned completely for the probable wisdom of human dealings.

Age is concerned with the wonderful because it stands near death, and with the probable because it can look back personally on the course of life. With the prospect of eternity, life in time appears ephemeral and evanescent, like a mirror (to which Alcidamas compared the *Odyssey*) or a dream. Longinus notes that creative geniuses have a tendency in old age to tell fables. Prospero, like Shakespeare, always shows the greatest respect for social decorum and breeding. Again and again he insists to Miranda and Ferdinand that they give not too much rein to dalliance. Yet during the formalized harvest ritual of the masque (with much in this play, very like the pastoral tradition), he utters his most wonderful statement, the justly famous passage which presents in sum the complete view of serene comedy toward art and life:

> *Our revels now are ended. These our actors,*
> *As I foretold you, were all spirits, and*
> *Are melted into air, into thin air;*
> *And, like the baseless fabric of this vision,*
> *The cloud-capp'd towers, the gorgeous palaces,*
> *The solemn temples, the great globe itself,*
> *Yea, all which it inherit, shall dissolve*
> *And, like the insubstantial pageant faded,*
> *Leave not a rack behind. We are such stuff*
> *As dreams are made on, and our little life*
> *Is rounded with a sleep.*

Afterword

The same human circumstance which makes me the custodian of the young man's book here reissued also makes it impossible for me to discuss its topics with him. And I still respect his views too much to alter them in his ineluctable absence.

From what I remember of him, I am sure he would resist any qualifications but a single one he wished to make himself. But he would welcome the few corrections of fact I have made for him. There would be no point in expanding his views on Homer here, since I have done so at considerable length in *The Classic Line,* a book I like to think he could have learned from. For some time I have been convinced that he radically misinterprets Don Quixote, but his view is a defensible one, and it has recently been defended in a doctoral thesis on Cervantes. What is worse, I find him quite imperceptive about Aristophanes, in whose writing he misses entirely the peerless blend of bold emblematic fantasy and lucid social analysis.

Into this wrongheaded emphasis, and into other simplifications, he was led by his headlong singlemindedness. That singlemindedness, however, gives his book whatever point it has. I remain convinced enough by it myself to send it out again in fresh dress, with gratitude both to its sympathetic new publishers and to the original press whose faith in a somewhat strange manuscript endowed a book with life and its author with a crucial reassurance.

ALBERT COOK

Buffalo, New York
June, 1966

Index